MICKEY LAWLER'S
SKYQUILTS

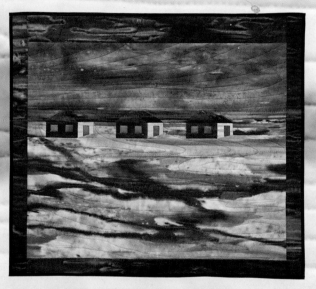

12 PAINTING TECHNIQUES
• CREATE DYNAMIC LANDSCAPE QUILTS

C&T PUBLISHING

Text copyright © 2011 by Mickey Lawler

Photography and artwork copyright © 2011 by C&T Publishing, Inc.

Photography copyright © 2011 by Jack McConnell

Publisher: Amy Marson

Creative Director: Gailen Runge

Acquisitions Editor: Susanne Woods

Editor: Lynn Koolish

Technical Editors: Ann Haley and Carolyn Aune

Cover Designer: Kristen Yenche

Book Designer: Christina D. Jarumay

Production Coordinator: Jessica Jenkins

Production Editors: Julia Cianci and S. Michele Fry

Illustrator: Kirstie Pettersen

Quilt Photography by Christina Carty-Francis and Diane Pedersen of C&T Publishing, Inc., unless otherwise noted

How-to Photography by Jack McConnell, unless otherwise noted

Published by C&T Publishing, Inc., P.O. Box 1456, Lafayette, CA 94549

Library of Congress Cataloging-in-Publication Data

Lawler, Mickey, 1940-
  Mickey Lawler's skyquilts : 12 painting techniques : create dynamic landscape quilts / Mickey Lawler.
    p. cm.
  ISBN 978-1-60705-243-2 (soft cover)
  1. Machine quilting. 2. Landscapes in art. 3. Textile painting. 4. Patchwork quilts. I. Title. II. Title: Skyquilts.
  TT835.L3785 2011
  746.46--dc22
                                    2010054236

Printed in China

10 9 8 7 6 5 4 3 2 1

CONTENTS

DEDICATION

*I dedicate this book to my three adult
daughters, Mary, Terry, and Katy.
I am constantly grateful and humbled
to have such beautiful spirits in my life.
And I also devote this book to the
thousands of quiltmaking students
and customers whose inspiration,
laughter, and encouragement have
nurtured me through the years.*

IN GRATITUDE

It has been a pleasure to work with all the wonderful
people at C&T Publishing once again. I am particularly
grateful to my editor, Lynn Koolish, for all her help and
encouragement, as well as to Diane Pedersen and the
entire production staff. Thank you all.

For great talent, gentle encouragement, and
generosity, I owe two dear friends, photographer
Jack McConnell (www.stonewalljack.com) and his wife
and business guru, Paula McNamara, of McConnell/
McNamara, enormous thanks, as well as my undying
devotion and admiration.

And to Sandy Birner, Jack's digital assistant, for your
patience, knowledge, and smiles through many hours
of "tech" stuff, thank you, thank you!

My humble thanks and much love throughout many
years to my dear quilting friends Carole Carter, Pam
Hardiman, Trish Hodge, MaryLyn Leander, Jean
Thibodeau, and Claire Wills, who have enthusiastically
made quilts for this book.

And to my pal Stevii Graves, for her sense of humor, in
her quilts and in life.

To my artists' group—Donna Donovan, Marsha Lewis,
Paula McNamara, Marlene Mayes, Rita Sobel, and
Linda Tajirian—many thanks for your artistic insights
and your dedication to work that inspires us all.

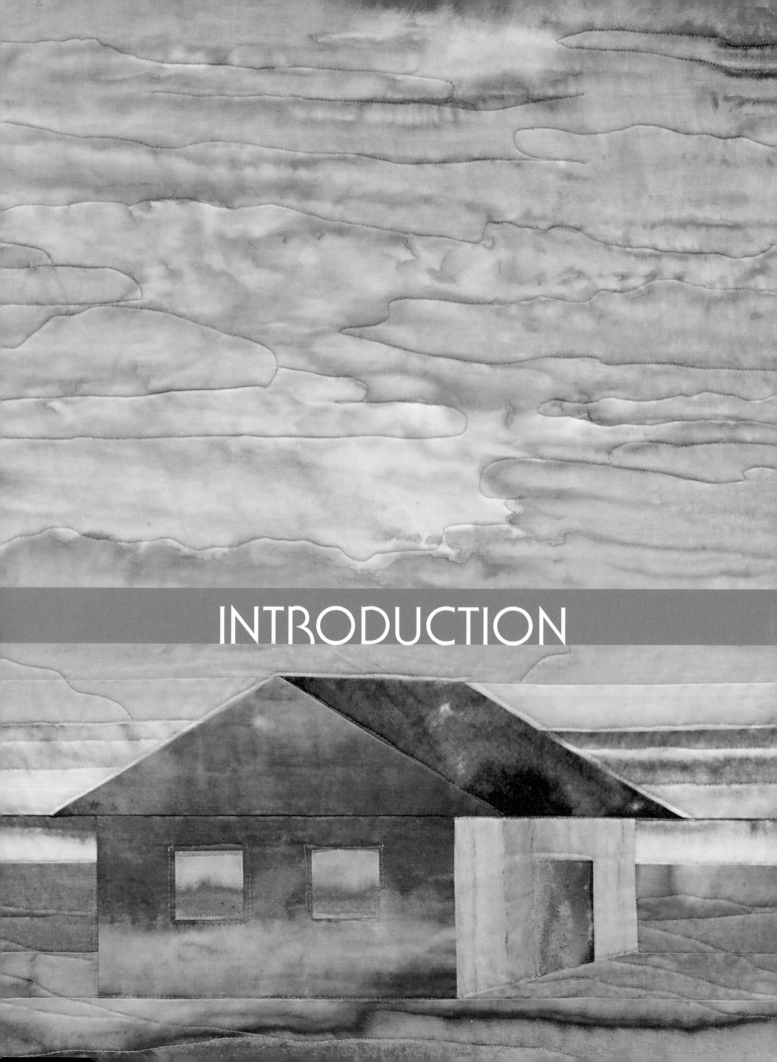

INTRODUCTION

USING YOUR PAINTED FABRIC FOR A SKYQUILT

The sky has a magic about it. Do you remember lying on your back on the cool grass, watching summer clouds drifting along in slow motion, and feeling yourself lifted up as if you had become part of the vast sky above? Wherever we are on this planet, the sky surrounds, inspires, sometimes awes, and often gentles us.

Photo by Jack McConnell

Photo by Jack McConnell

An African folktale about indigo dye tells us that long ago the sky was more important than just a place to rest our eyes. Sky could be eaten and would fill up hearts and stomachs. Pieces of clouds lodged inside a person would cause happiness and lovely dreams. The diner had to be pure in thought to be a good Sky-eater and might even become silly or drunk from consuming too much. Imperfect Sky-eating, however, often brought tragic results. Saddened by this devastation, and not wanting to cause more heartache, Sky pulled itself up higher where it could not be reached. Out of compassion though, Sky gave women the secret of its blue to make beautiful cloth for people so they could be happy again and would have less need to eat Sky.

Photo by Jack McConnell

I have been painting sky- and landscape-style fabrics and making quilts for several decades, a life's work that continues to surprise me. As a quiltmaker, I began painting fabric to satisfy my own need for skies and other landscape elements that were sorely lacking in commercial textiles. I found that many quiltmakers had the same need, so my passion merged into my business, and SKYDYES was born.

"I've bought SKYDYES fabric from you for ten years; I can't bring myself to cut it, but I'm sure I need more!"

A woman approached me with those words at a quilt show not too long ago. We laughed together, but frankly I wasn't surprised. While I continued to make quilts from my fabric, I began to realize that many of my customers were putting their SKYDYES fabrics on a special shelf and taking them out to pat once in awhile, because the fabrics were "too precious" to cut. I had heard variations of that woman's sentiment for years.

From the beginning I have painted fabric with the intention that it will be cut and used in quilts. In my mind the fabric is a tool and its purpose incomplete until it is used. I know most quilters have a devotion to wonderful fabric, and I confess that I have a hard time snipping some fabrics into pieces. Naturally, those utilitarian leafy greens and garden colors are no problem; they are easily cut. But what about an exquisite sky? Who can imagine cutting a piece out of the middle of that beautiful yard of fabric? I admit I used to feel the same. So, instead of hoarding my favorites or watching my rotary cutter shake as I was about to slice, I began to give those fabrics starring roles and to let them shine.

Although the reflections in the water are pieced, I fused the buildings onto a subdued autumn sky and then fused tiny, well-chosen pieces for windows. Paint that had mistakenly dripped down the edges of a fabric became a subtle tree.

West Side November, by Mickey Lawler, 31" × 42", 2000

In 2000, I started using only one or two sky fabrics for my quilts. *West Side November*, which shows a view across the Hudson River to the west side of Manhattan on a gray November day, was preceded by one of my paper collages. The quilt was created using painted fabric and is fused, pieced, and machine quilted. The sky dictated the mood and guided my choice of fabric colors for the buildings and foreground.

Boreas, by Mickey Lawler, 41″ × 52″, 2003

For my quilt *Boreas*, which is named for the Greek god of the cold north wind, I cut several large sections of only two skies resembling an aurora. The quilt is composed entirely of my painted fabric. It is machine pieced and machine quilted.

Design Strip

Then one day I designed a quilt inspired by the little cottages lined up on a narrow strip of sand between Cape Cod Bay and the Atlantic Ocean. The design was so linear that it occurred to me all I had to do was piece the cottages into a *design strip* and add a wholecloth painted sky and a wholecloth painted foreground to have a beautiful finished quilt top.

Painting fabric, by its very nature, demands that I suspend complete control over the result—trying to paint just the right piece of fabric with a quilt already in mind can be far too frustrating. Instead, when I decide to make a new quilt, I look to my shelves of painted fabric and sort through favorite pieces until one cries out to be used. I have always made quilts this way, starting with a beautiful piece of fabric and building a quilt around it.

Because my painted skies have always offered inspiration—and a starting point—for my quilts, I began to think of them as *SkyQuilts*. In this book I've shared some of my methods for painting fabric and suggested a few projects to help you get started on quilts using the *design strip* technique. I hope you enjoy this worry-free process for making beautiful quilts.

Imagine the possibilities!

Beach Houses 1, by Mickey Lawler, 56″ × 48″, 2006

I immediately loved the ease of this process. For me, it was perfect. I could select a favorite sky, pair it with a landscape fabric for the foreground, and design a strip as a focus to fit the scene.

TOOLS AND EQUIPMENT
FOR PAINTING FABRIC

Most of the equipment you will need for painting fabric is inexpensive and easy to find in local stores, with the exception of the fabric paints. You may be able to find fabric paint in a local art supply store, or check the Resources section (page 94) for online and mail-order suppliers of quality fabric paints.

You will need:

- Fabric paints in your choice of basic colors

- Containers for mixing paints

- Brushes

- A couple of large natural sponges

- A spray bottle with a good mist setting

- A bottle or pitcher to hold clear water for mixing

- Rubber gloves, if you desire

- A roll of paper towels, just in case

- Good-quality white 100% cotton fabric

- A plastic-covered surface on which to paint

Tools for successful fabric painting

PAINTS

The most important considerations when choosing water-based fabric paints are quality, permanence, and whether the paints do what you want them to do. The paints should work well on any natural fiber (cotton, silk, and so on) and be permanent when dried and heat set. Diluted paints shouldn't change the hand, or feel, of the fabric very much. It's a good idea to check the manufacturer's website to make sure the paints are nontoxic.

Paint quality can often be judged by how much the paints cost. Unlike many other items on which we spend money, the price you pay for paint reflects the quality. Good pigment, or the particles of pure color, is expensive. The more pigment a paint manufacturer uses, the more expensive the paint. However, an expensive paint may actually be more economical because you'll need to use less paint when you dilute it to get a lighter color.

TIP

Don't confuse paints with dyes. Dyes have an entirely different chemical makeup and are not used in this book.

Transparent fabric paints are best for a watercolor look on your fabric. Transparent paints come from the manufacturer as very thick liquid, and most should be diluted somewhat before using. I often dilute my paint with *one part water to one part paint* and use this diluted paint as my *base mixture*, diluting further as needed. The paints should flow nicely when water or extender/medium is added, allowing colors to move into one another to create complexity; this technique should result in a translucent effect on the finished fabric. Transparent paint will not completely cover other colors or designs already on the fabric.

The transparent paints I prefer are:

- PROfab Textile Paint transparent from PRO Chemical and Dye

- Setacolor Transparent Paint

- Liquitex Soft Body (transparent colors), to be used with Liquitex's fabric medium

- Jacquard Textile Colors (semiopaque)

Metallic and pearlescent fabric paints are generally opaque and can be used to cover other colors already on the fabric, or they can be mixed with transparent paints for a bit of sparkle. I prefer to mix them into my other paints; only occasionally do I use them alone. These paints can be diluted as much as you like, from using a good amount of water for a light shimmer to using only a small amount of water for a heavy metal look.

The metallic paints I prefer are:

- Jacquard Lumiere

- PRObrite Textile Paint from PRO Chemical and Dye

- Liquitex Iridescent Colors

To add a really intense color here and there, I love using Createx Airbrush Colors in both regular colors and metallics. I dilute them with a bit of water and paint them on the fabric with a brush, as I would any of the transparent paints.

Opaque fabric paints are good for details when you want more control and don't want the paint to flow. For example, if you want to paint the windows and doors on your *Beach Houses* quilt (page 55) or add grasses or rocks to a finished painted fabric, opaque paints are a good choice. They cover colors and designs already on the fabric. I usually don't dilute my opaque paints more than one part water to three parts paint to make sure I retain the opacity. Test any opaque fabric paints before using, as some can give a chalky look to the finished piece.

The opaque paints I prefer are:

- Jacquard Neopaque

- Setacolor Opaque

- Liquitex Soft Body (opaque colors), to be used with Liquitex's fabric medium

The water, sky, and reflections in this piece of fabric were first painted with *transparent* and *metallic* paints. After they were dry, I added the wood pilings with *opaque* paints.

Sources for paints are included in Resources (page 94).

MIXING COLORS

Each brand of paint offers slightly different variations of the basic primary colors (red, yellow, blue), secondary colors (green, orange, violet), and tertiary colors (blue-violet, red-violet, blue-green, yellow-green, red-orange, yellow-orange). Making your own color chart, based on the brand of paint you're using, is a very good idea, as this cuts down on the time you will spend mixing a new combination, especially if you're a beginning fabric painter.

This simple color chart will help get you started. However, the colors on your own chart may vary a bit, depending on the brand and your choices. More complex color charts can be purchased at any art supply store.

> **TIP**
>
> *A warm blue tends more toward green; a cool blue is more violet. In the same way, a warm red will tend toward orange, and a cool red, again, toward violet.*

COLOR CHART

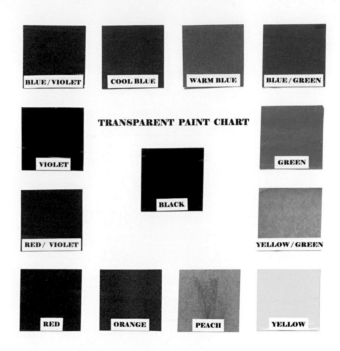

BROWN & BLACK MIXING CHART
(TRANSPARENT PAINTS)

OPAQUE METALLICS

Painted color chart

Assuming you have made a *base mixture* of one part water to one part paint of the twelve basic paints on the chart, you will usually need to dilute further. Unless stated, the combinations that follow are about one part *base mixture* paint to one part water. Test the colors you mix on a piece of *test cloth* and adjust the ratio of paint to water as needed.

TO GET	MIX
Blue-green	Warm blue + green (Using more green than blue will result in a turquoise color.)
Blue-violet	Cool blue + violet
Bright blue	Cool blue + warm blue
Brown-black	Any brown on the color chart + a few drops of black
Dark cool blue	Cool blue + a couple drops of black
Dark gray	Black + a few drops of cool blue + extra water as needed
Deep forest-green	Green + a few drops of red (and perhaps black)
Gold	Yellow + a few drops of violet
Gray	Black + a few drops of cool blue + extra water as needed
Gray-violet	Violet + a few drops of black
Hot orange	Red + yellow
Light green	Green + extra water
Pale cool blue	Cool blue + extra water for diluting
Peach	Yellow + a few drops of red
Red-violet	Red + violet
Sandy brown	Yellow + violet, adjusting amounts of each color as needed
Warm brown	Orange + blue
Yellow-green	Yellow + green

To make colors lighter, add more water, an *extender*, or a *medium* (see Tip, page 13) if the brand you are using suggests this. For some brands of paint, using an extender is better than adding water to avoid weakening the permanence of the paint.

To keep colors intense, use very little water—just enough so that the paint will not be too stiff, sticky, or gummy when it dries.

To tone down colors, add a few drops of the color's complement. Complements are colors that are across from each other on the color wheel, such as red and green, violet and yellow, and blue and orange. If you aren't sure what a color's complement is, use a color tool such as the 3-in-1 Color Tool (www.ctpub.com).

The 3-in-1 Color Tool makes it easy to find complementary colors.

Be sure to take time to practice mixing colors before you paint; I often spend far more time mixing my colors than I do actually painting the fabric. *Always, always* test your colors on a piece of *test cloth* to be sure they are what you hoped. The test cloth should be the same fabric, either dampened or dry, on which you will be painting. Test all the colors side by side for the piece you plan to paint. Looking at a color in isolation won't give you a good basis for a decision about how it may look surrounded by others. Allow the paint to dry, so you can see the true color.

Containers for Mixing Paints

Old, clean plastic recycled deli-style or yogurt containers will be fine for mixing paints. Paint adheres to some types of plastics, so you may have to discard them after a few uses.

BRUSHES AND SPONGES

You don't have to spend a lot of money on brushes. Simple natural-bristle brushes from a hardware store or a dollar store are fine. These often have the words *natural bristle* printed on the wooden handle. Sponge brushes also come in handy for some applications. Buy a few sizes of each type of brush, so that you don't have to wash them between colors. I suggest three to four 3″, 2″, and 1″ brushes. You may also want to have a ½″ watercolor brush on hand for fine details. If you decide to make the City stencil (pattern pullout page P-2), you will also need a stencil brush. This round brush, which has short, stiff bristles designed just for this type of work, can be found in art or craft supply stores.

I like to use natural sponges for some skies because they give a light, airy look to clouds. If you have a hard time finding natural sponges, some good artificial sponges are on the market now. Whichever you choose, try to find sponges that have large holes, are somewhat flat

on one side, and are about the size of your hand. When I travel, I seek out art supply stores on my quest to find the next perfect sponge.

SPRAY BOTTLE

While a small cosmetic spray bottle may be sufficient for dampening small pieces of fabric, indulge in a pump sprayer for larger pieces. Not only does it save wear and tear on your hand muscles, but also most have a very fine mist setting. These bottles are not expensive and can be found in the garden section of your hardware or home improvement store.

FABRIC

A good smooth 100% white cotton fabric is extremely important. You will get the best results by using a tightly woven fabric, like a broadcloth or Egyptian cotton (which, sadly, isn't actually made in Egypt any longer). The reason for this is that the more threads there are per inch, the more paint will be held on the surface of your fabric, rather than seeping between the fibers. If paint seeps between the fibers, the result will be a dull, washed-out piece. The threads of the fabric should also be fine and smooth. Heavy threads absorb more paint and can interrupt the flow of your painted design. White cotton, rather than off-white, will give you the most accurate colors. An off-white cotton will tone down colors, much like adding a bit of brown to each of your paints.

The fabric does not necessarily have to be PFD (prepared for dyeing). A good test of whether certain fabrics will work for painting is to buy a small amount of several fabrics, take them home, and then label and paint each. Let them all dry and then decide.

Some sources of good fabric are included in Resources (page 94).

WORK SPACES

I paint fabric almost year-round and keep two studios, one outdoors in summer and another indoors in winter. There are advantages and disadvantages to both spaces.

My favorite place to paint fabric is outdoors in the sunshine on a bright summer day. Here in the Northeast, my outdoor painting season is usually from May through September. I'm envious of my California friends who can paint outdoors whenever the mood strikes. The disadvantage of painting outdoors in my area is the changeable weather. I have become an amateur meteorologist, watching the weather patterns every day, and often judging how much time I have before thunderclouds arrive.

Although I have a very small yard, each spring I set up my long painting tables in a private spot amid my gardens and patio. While the fabrics are drying, I can sit down with a cool drink or do a little weeding.

I love painting outdoors in the garden.

For the cold months, I have an indoor space set up with bright lights, heaters, and gentle blowers. This space has its benefits also. I don't have to worry about a sudden rain shower washing away my hard work or mosquitoes feasting on my ankles. Several years ago, I had new heating ducts installed with blowers above each painting table. Even with that, the paints never dry as quickly indoors, so I have to adjust my paints by adding less water. In addition, excellent artificial lights and heat never quite reproduce the natural light and heat of the summer sun.

Setting Up a Painting Area

All you need is an 8´ × 12´ space to call your own and some inexpensive items available at a home improvement center. In this size space, and with the following equipment, you can paint 45˝-wide fabric up to about 2 yards long.

- A pair of sawhorses (I still use the same sawhorses I bought fifteen years ago.)

- A 4´ × 8´ piece of insulation board about 1˝ thick (not Styrofoam)

- A couple of 8´-long metal supports of some kind

- Plastic or contact paper for covering insulation board

- Duct tape to secure insulation board to the sawhorses in case of wind

If you will be painting indoors, add some good color-rendering (full-spectrum) fluorescent lights over your work space, and try to choose a spot that will give you the driest heat. A standing fan may help.

To save wear and tear on your back, you may want to build up the height of your sawhorses by adding wide boards. After one week of an aching back, I added additional boards to give me the desired height.

Add boards to sawhorses, if needed, to provide a comfortable height for your painting.

Insulation board is lightweight and inexpensive, and it makes a great rigid surface on which to paint. However, it can get dented and gouged easily; so after a couple of seasons, you will probably need to replace it. I have no idea what the long metal supports in the photo below are called, but I bought them and the insulation board at my home improvement center. The supports provide further rigidity and keep my insulation board from sagging if I paint too energetically.

Adding metal supports keeps the insulation board from sagging.

Cover the insulation board with plastic or contact paper to provide a smooth surface for painting. You can find various weights of 48″-wide plastic, usually on rolls and sold by the yard, at a decorator fabric store. The added benefit of either plastic or contact paper is that you never have to wash off the surface after painting. Once the paint is dry, it will not rewet onto the next piece of fabric you put down. I just wipe down my painting surface each morning to clear the dust away. Usually I can paint about 1,000 yards of fabric before I have to re-cover the insulation board, and the only reason I have to do that is because the surface eventually becomes a bit sticky with built-up paint.

Cover insulation board with plastic for a painting surface.

Be sure to tape, or somehow secure, the insulation board to the sawhorses. I leave my painting tables outside for months; however, having learned from experience, I place a couple bricks on top if I know a storm is coming. Looking outside to see your insulation board crumpled in a neighbor's yard is not a great way to begin the day!

If you have very little space in which to paint, a tabletop and a piece of foamcore board covered with plastic will work just fine. Foamcore board is a nice, rigid surface and can easily be carried outdoors. The only drawback is that your painted fabric will be limited to the size of the foamcore board. The painting exercises in this book are about 22″ × 30″, so a piece of foamcore approximately 30″ × 40″ and about ¼″ thick will be fine. These boards are available at most office supply or art supply stores.

Now that you have a pleasant area for painting and all the supplies on hand, there are just one or two more things to consider before you dive in!

BEFORE YOU BEGIN

By now you have all the equipment you need to paint fabric. But before you have that overwhelming urge to pick up those brushes and plunge right in, take a moment to look over these basic hints to help you succeed. Knowing the following information ahead of time, and referring to it as you go through the exercises, will give you a solid foundation for the enjoyment of painting on fabric.

FABRIC

It's a good idea to start with manageable-sized pieces. The fabric in the following photos is about 30˝ × 22˝. This is a great size to start with—it's easy to handle but large enough to use in a wall quilt. As you become comfortable with the process, you may want to work on much larger pieces.

MIXING PAINTS

After you have decided on colors and mixed your paints (pages 14-16), always test them together on a test cloth. Be sure to use the same fabric on which you will be painting. If directions call for painting on damp fabric, dampen the test cloth. Test paints on a dry piece if you will be painting on dry fabric. Testing is *essential* to give you an accurate view of how the colors will look together and to let you know whether you need to tweak a color, add another color, or discard one entirely. However, do not discard your test cloth. I have yards of test cloths in my mixing area that have often come in handy when I need a small piece of fabric for my quilts.

PAINTING ON DAMP FABRIC

Place the fabric on your painting surface (page 17), and mist gently with water to completely dampen the fabric's surface.

Fabric for all dampened pieces should not be too saturated. A good test is to lay your bare hand on the damp fabric. Now look at the palm of your hand. If you see puddles of water on your hand, the fabric is too wet. Simply use some paper towels to absorb the excess water. The fabric should be evenly damp but not soggy. Smooth the fabric with your hand. A few T-pins are helpful to hold the fabric in place while you paint.

PAINTING ON DRY FABRIC

Stretch a piece of fabric on your painting surface, making sure there are no wrinkles or fold lines. A few T-pins are helpful to hold the fabric in place here as well.

The same colors were painted on both a damp and a dry piece of fabric. There are times when both applications are desirable.

DRYING THE PAINTED FABRIC

Painted fabric must be allowed to dry flat. Remember that you are working with paints not dyes, so tilting the fabric or hanging it will cause the paints to run off the surface. The faster the paint dries, the more the paint will stay on the surface of the fabric fibers, instead of sinking in and losing the colors. Painted fabrics will almost always dry to a lighter shade than how they appear when you first apply the paint. I get the best results by drying my fabrics outdoors in the sun. When this isn't possible, I work under heat lamps. Only use a hair dryer if it has a diffuser; the force of the air coming directly from the hair dryer can move the wet paint around or push it further into the fibers of the fabric.

And, no, **never** dry painted fabric in your clothes dryer—unless you want very pale fabric and a very colorful dryer!

SETTING THE COLORS

The most secure method for ensuring that the paints are permanent on your fabric is to heat set the fabric by ironing it slowly on a hot cotton setting for a couple of minutes. This will bond a good-quality paint to the fibers. Be sure that your painted fabric is absolutely dry before ironing. I generally wait a few days before heat setting, just to be safe. I have never needed to use a pressing cloth between the fabric and my iron, but it's an individual choice. A pressing cloth may make sense for those who may be a bit cautious at first. Some brands of paints don't need to be heat set, so when in doubt, follow the manufacturer's directions.

PAINTING FABRIC
FOR A SKYQUILT

This chapter covers a number of techniques to paint fabric for skies and foregrounds. The next chapter covers special techniques to paint fabric for details or focal points that make the final work interesting and exciting.

If you are a newcomer to painting, be gentle with yourself. Take time to feel at home with the paints. Setting a goal of painting eight to ten skies and foregrounds will give you enough experience to raise your comfort level considerably. The added benefit is that the more pieces you paint, the more choices you will have for inspiration. The danger, on the other hand, is that you will love painting fabric so much that you'll never make another quilt!

SKIES

Most artists recognize that the way a sky is painted determines the mood and lighting of the entire piece, as it will in your SkyQuilt. A clear sky means it is a sunny day, perhaps early to mid afternoon. The mood is light and airy. The colors in the rest of the quilt should reflect that mood—clear, nothing too somber, except maybe a few shadows to indicate the strong sun of summer.

Sunset scenes may give the feeling of peace and serenity. Of course, there are exceptions. Stormy skies speak of excitement and action. I have always loved painting skies—they tell me what my quilts should be.

Beach Houses 1, by Mickey Lawler, 56″ × 48″, 2006

The subject matter is often a pleasant, uplifting scene.

Beach Houses 2, by Mickey Lawler, 37″ × 33″, 2007

On the other hand, a moody sky with grayed colors creates a sense of drama and may call for darker tones in the foreground.

BLUE SKIES

The simplest sky to paint is a blue sky with a few white clouds, a staple for any landscape quilter. It's also a great beginner's project to conquer the fear of putting paint on perfectly good white fabric.

Supplies

See Tools and Equipment for Painting Fabric (pages 11–18) for information on paint and supplies.

- Cool blue transparent paint
- Warm blue transparent paint
- White opaque paint (optional)
- Large natural sponge (an additional sponge is needed if using optional white opaque paint)
- 2 containers for mixing the paints, large enough to accommodate the sponge
- Misting spray bottle
- White fabric
- Brush to test paint when mixing

Mixing Paints

1. Refer to the Color Chart (page 14) to help decide on the 2 blues.

2. Dilute each paint color with at least an equal amount of water.

3. Test the 2 colors on a dampened test cloth.

If the colors are too intense, add more water. If the colors are too pale, add more paint. Keep testing the colors until they are to your satisfaction. Remember that the paint will be lighter after it has dried because the amount of dampness on the fabric will dilute the colors to some degree.

Painting a Blue Sky

1. Dampen the fabric.

2. Dip the sponge into one of the paints, squeezing out just enough excess paint so it doesn't drip on the cloth by accident.

3. Lightly *bounce* the sponge on the dampened fabric, leaving white areas to suggest clouds. On damp fabric, the paint will continue to move, so be sure to leave enough white.

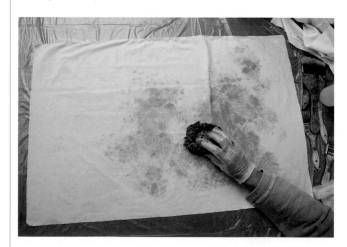

4. Repeat for the second blue, overlapping the first blue here and there. It's fine to use the same sponge for both blues, as the blending will give an added complexity to the piece.

5. For more prominent clouds, mix opaque white with a little water. Use a clean sponge to apply it to the existing white areas, using a bit more pressure than you used for the blue.

6. Allow the fabric to dry flat.

Because the fabric was too damp, this sky became quite pale. Yet it turned out to have a very ethereal look and will be a wonderful sky for some quilt in the future.

Streaking paints horizontally across the fabric with a sponge creates a quieter, more static sky.

SUNSET

Sunsets around the world appear in many different colors, more than you might realize. The word *sunset* generally brings to mind purples, reds, oranges, blues, and golds. However, take a look at some of the old masters' paintings, and you'll see that there are often different shades of brown in their sunsets, a color we don't usually associate with sunsets. In reality, there are browns in many sunsets where two complementary colors, such as blue and orange, come together. Our visual brain just doesn't make the distinction. No color is truly out of bounds when you are making color choices.

An easy way to begin is to decide whether you would like your sunset to be primarily warm or cool colors.

Primarily warm colors with a cool complement

Warm sunset colors

Cool sunset colors

When mixing and testing colors for your sunset, you might find that adding a complement will enhance your selection. For example, a peachy yellow sky is far more interesting with a few streaks of violet.

For this exercise, I chose to paint warm colors near the horizon, moving upward to cool colors.

Supplies

See Tools and Equipment for Painting Fabric (pages 11-18) for information on paint and supplies.

- Hot orange transparent paint
- Red transparent paint
- Bright blue transparent paint
- Violet transparent paint
- Yellow opaque paint (optional)
- Gold or pearl metallic paint (optional)
- 3 or 4 brushes
- 4 containers for mixing paints
- Misting spray bottle
- White fabric

Mixing Paints

1. Refer to Mixing Colors (pages 14-16) to mix the 4 transparent colors in the 4 containers, adding only a small amount of water so the colors will be vibrant.

2. Test the colors on a damp test cloth.

Are the colors what you envisioned? If the orange is too yellow, add a few more drops of red. Or if the purple is too red, add a few more drops of blue. Keep tweaking the colors until you are happy with the combination. The time it takes to do this is well worth the effort.

Painting a Sunset

1. Dampen the fabric (page 20).

2. Starting at the bottom of the fabric, brush on the warm colors in both long and short strokes.

Note: To give a more natural look when painting a horizontal sky, make sure the strokes of color are uneven as you work across the fabric.

3. Paint in some purples and blues.

Adding to a Sunset

After the fabric is dry, you might like to add a sun or moon to the scene.

1. Mix a yellow *opaque* paint with a little gold or pearl metallic and test on a dry piece of fabric.

Note: *Do not dampen* the fabric this time. Painting on dry fabric will allow the sun to retain sharp edges and not bleed into the sky.

2. Using a 1″ foam brush, apply a small amount of paint by twisting the brush in a circular motion onto the fabric.

Don't be discouraged if your sun is not perfectly round the first time. Just go back over it.

It's okay if the sun becomes a bit larger each time.

STORMY SKY

Stormy skies are painted in a manner similar to the technique used for sunsets—the only difference is the colors.

Supplies

See Tools and Equipment for Painting Fabric (pages 11-18) for information on paint and supplies. Refer to Mixing Colors (pages 14-16) for information on mixing paints.

- Pale cool blue transparent paint
- Dark cool blue transparent paint
- Dark gray transparent paint
- Blue-violet transparent paint
- 3 or 4 brushes
- Large sponge (optional)
- 4 containers for mixing paints
- Misting spray bottle
- White fabric

Mixing Paints

1. To make a pale cool blue, add enough water to create a light tone.

2. Keep the dark cool blue, dark gray, and blue-violet fairly intense by adding only a small amount of water.

3. Test the colors on a dampened test cloth.

Painting a Stormy Sky

1. Dampen the fabric (page 20).

2. Stroke the pale cool blue in a random pattern onto the fabric.

3. Continue with the other colors, covering some of the pale cool blue.

Note: Because stormy skies don't have the gentle, horizontal look of a sunset, try to keep the strokes energetic and irregular.

FOREGROUNDS

Now you are faced with another decision: What do you place in the foreground or bottom portion of your quilt? Will this quilt be a landscape or seascape? Is this a day-time scene or evening? What is the mood of the scene? (Remember that the sky you have chosen will direct the mood of the quilt.) If you're planning a seascape, is the water calm or turbulent?

Calm water

Turbulent water

For a landscape quilt, there are other factors to consider: Rolling hills? A garden? Sandy beaches? Long scenic vistas? So many possibilities!

How important will the foreground be in the finished quilt? Perhaps you want to emphasize the sky and only intend to use a narrow section of foreground. You may not be able to answer all these questions until you have finished painting several skies and foregrounds.

> ✳ *My best advice is to try many skies and fore-grounds and then decide which ones make you happy and lead you to a new quilt.*

WATER

Why is it that we are drawn to this source of life? Poets, composers, and visual artists have been inspired for centuries by the romantic, the peaceful, the powerful, or, sometimes, the dangerous allure of water. We have always had an innate attraction to and love of water beyond mere survival. Just try to lure a two-year-old away from the sink or kiddie pool! Like all living organisms, water moves and changes. The sea constantly ebbs and flows, and even the quietest pool sways imperceptibly with the earth and the breezes.

Color choices for water cover most of the cool spectrum: blues, grays, greens, violets. Try substituting any of these for the colors listed in this exercise and you'll see some very different results.

Supplies

See Tools and Equipment for Painting Fabric (pages 11-18) for information on paint and supplies. Refer to Mixing Colors (pages 14-16) for information on mixing paints.

- Cool blue transparent paint
- Warm blue transparent paint
- Blue-green transparent paint
- 1 or 2 brushes
- 3 containers for mixing paint
- Misting spray bottle
- White fabric (2 pieces)

Mixing Paints

1. For an intense Aegean Sea blue, add only a small amount of water to the paints. For the softer colors of a pond, add a bit more water to the paints. Mixing a blue that is lighter than the others will give depth to the finished painting.

2. Test the colors on a dampened test cloth.

Painting Calm Water

I've discovered that by using a second layer of fabric, I can easily create water that is either turbulent or quiet and yet still conveys movement.

1. Place a piece of fabric on your painting surface and dampen.

2. Ripple the fabric in a somewhat horizontal manner; then place a second piece of fabric on top. The top layer will not be rippled.

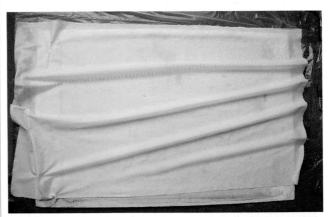

3. Stroke the paints onto the top fabric in a horizontal fashion. As you do this, you will see the texture of the folds from the ripples begin to appear.

4. When you're finished painting, don't separate the fabrics. Allow them to dry together.

The top layer will remain more intense in color.

Often the bottom layer turns out to be a very wonderful and usable fabric. This is the bottom layer of the piece I had just finished.

TIP

Spraying the bottom layer with salted water will result in more swirls and waves. I usually add about ¼ cup of table salt to about 3 quarts of warm water and stir or shake the solution until the salt is completely dissolved.

REFLECTIONS ON THE WATER

Taking a lead from one of the sunset skies that you painted, you may want to incorporate some of the sunset colors into a water piece to create reflections.

Colors from a cool sunset are reflected in the water.

Supplies

See Tools and Equipment for Painting Fabric (pages 11-18) for information on paint and supplies.

- Blue-violet transparent paint
- Red-violet transparent paint
- Cool blue transparent paint
- Warm blue transparent paint
- Blue-green transparent paint
- 3 or 4 brushes
- Containers for mixing paints
- Misting spray bottle
- White fabric (2 pieces)

Mixing Paints

1. Mix the blue paints in the same manner as you did for calm water (page 31).

2. Mix the violet combinations with about the same intensity as the blues. For example, if you are working with intense blues and using very little water to dilute the colors, dilute the 2 violets to the same degree.

3. Test the colors on a dampened test cloth.

Painting Reflections on Water

1. Prepare the fabric in the same manner as you did for calm water (page 31).

2. Brush the 2 violet paints with horizontal strokes in vertical rows down the damp fabric.

3. While the violets are still quite wet, use a brush to drag the blues across the violets at irregular intervals. This will allow some of the violets to be picked up and to move into the blues.

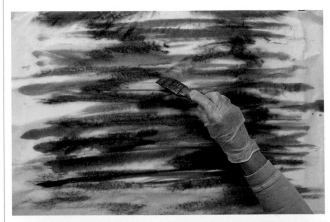

> **TIP**
>
> *Leaving some streaks of white will heighten the illusion of reflected light.*

LAND

I paint most of my land pieces in a manner similar to painting water. The difference, of course, lies in the colors. I like to paint random land pieces, using whatever colors inspire me that day. However, if you are planning a foreground to work well with one of your skies, try incorporating some of the sky colors into that foreground. For example, a dark sunset sky calls for more depth of color in the foreground and works best if some of the sunset colors are repeated in the foreground.

Foreground for a dark sunset sky

The deeper colors in this foreground echo a late afternoon sky. This might be a perfect combination for inserting a distant mountain design strip (page 50).

SAND

Desert or beach, sand is one of the easiest beginner paintings. There are only subtle variations in the colors, so no matter how you paint it, it will work as a sandy foreground.

The sandy foreground picks up colors from the sky.

Supplies

See Tools and Equipment for Painting Fabric (pages 11-18) for information on paint and supplies. Refer to Mixing Colors (pages 14-16) for information on mixing paints.

- Gold transparent paint
- Sandy brown transparent paint
- Warm brown transparent paint
- Gray transparent paint
- Gray-violet transparent paint
- Pearl metallic opaque paint (optional)
- 3 or 4 brushes
- Containers for mixing paints
- Misting spray bottle
- White fabric (2 pieces)

Mixing Paints

1. Keep the colors soft and light by adding enough water to each to dilute the intensity.

2. Test the colors on a dampened test cloth.

*Adding some pearl metallic or iridescent paints will **pastel** the colors and add sparkle to the sand.*

Painting Sand

1. Prepare the fabric in the same manner as you did for calm water (page 31).

2. Stroke the colors horizontally onto the fabric in random order.

3. Spatter a bit of slightly diluted pearl metallic paint to create additional texture in the sand.

Leaving some streaks of white implies a sunny day.

OTHER FOREGROUNDS

Combine water and sand to create more interest and provide a definite sense of place.

Sponge on colors from lightest to darkest to produce a sense of distance and depth.

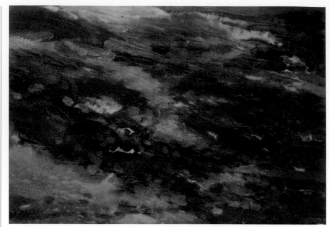

Try using both brushes and sponges in an energetic, diagonal direction for greater movement in a stylized garden.

This foreground and warm sunset sing a dynamic duet.

GREEN FIELDS

Planning landscapes wouldn't be complete without the greens of grassy meadows and forests.

Supplies

See Tools and Equipment for Painting Fabric (pages 11-18) for information on paint and supplies. Refer to Mixing Colors (pages 14-16) for information on mixing paints.

- Light green transparent paint
- Yellow-green transparent paint
- Blue-green transparent paint

- Deep forest green transparent paint
- Copper metallic opaque paint
- Gold metallic opaque paint
- 3 or 4 brushes
- Containers for mixing paints
- Misting spray bottle
- White fabric

Mixing Paints

1. Add some gold metallic to a couple of the greens for highlights in the finished piece.

2. As always, adding only a small amount of water to the paint will result in vibrant colors. For softer greens, add water until you get the shade you desire.

3. Test the colors on a dampened test cloth.

Painting Green Fields

1. Dampen the fabric (page 20).

2. Use a lot of paint for this application, completely covering the fabric.

3. Add streaks of copper metallic over the greens.

4. To create dark textured lines and to allow the paint to flow about randomly, gently pinch the wet painted fabric into folds.

5. Allow the paint to set in these folds for about a half hour, then pull the fabric flat and let it dry completely.

Turning the finished piece vertically presents all kinds of ideas for a new quilt. Perhaps a forest background?

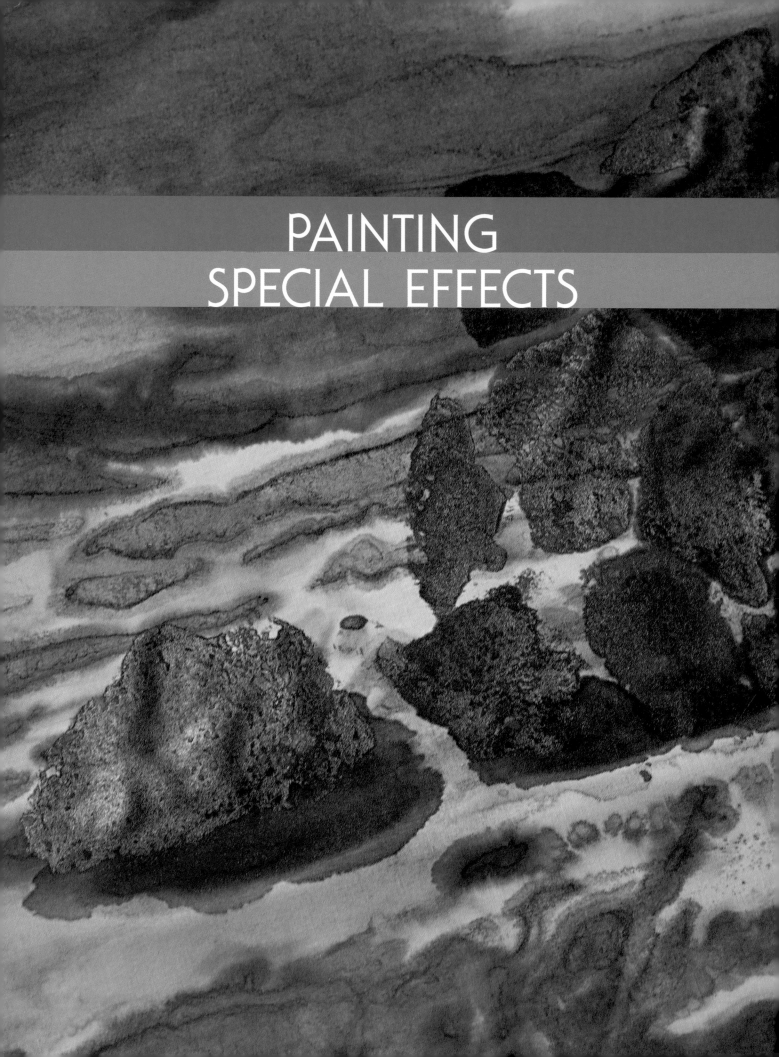

PAINTING
SPECIAL EFFECTS

I have tried literally dozens of different techniques for putting paint on fabric, many creating wonderful textures that I've found useful for my quilts. I've chosen five of the most popular for you to play around with, ranging from fast and easy to more advanced, but each well worth the time and effort.

SCRUNCH PAINTING

This fabric is stress-free and just plain fun to paint. It's a wonderful piece to cut up for leaves, rocks, flower petals, and loads of other features. Because each time the results are different, and often unexpected, I've had students who, once introduced to this technique, want nothing more than to spend a day painting dozens of them.

Supplies

See Tools and Equipment for Painting Fabric (pages 11-18) for information on paint and supplies.

- Black transparent paint
- Sandy brown transparent paint
- Warm brown transparent paint
- Gray transparent paint
- Pearl metallic opaque paint
- 3 or 4 brushes
- Containers for mixing paints
- Misting spray bottle
- White fabric

Mixing Paints

Refer to Mixing Colors (pages 14-16) for information on mixing paints.

1. Add some pearl metallic to a couple of your browns for highlights in the finished piece.

2. Test the colors on a dampened test cloth.

Painting Scrunch Fabric

Note: As in green fields (page 36), use a lot of paint for this application, completely covering the fabric.

1. Dampen the fabric.

2. To apply a good saturation of paint quickly, hold the paint container over your work. I have found that placing the container too far away from their work makes people worry about dripping paint and, therefore, prevents them from loading enough paint on the brush.

3. Keep adding colors at random; however, don't obliterate each color with the next.

4. When the fabric is completely covered with paint, scrunch it into tiny folds and allow the fabric to dry this way.

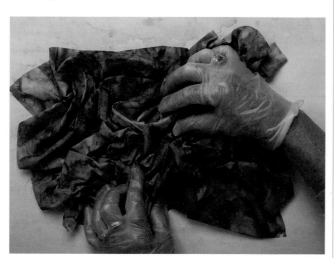

5. Once the fabric is dry, spread it flat.

6. If there are too many white spaces on the fabric, dampen the entire piece again and repeat the process.

Imagine the wonderful fabric you could create using rose-petal colors or leafy greens or only gold, silver, and bronze metallics.

BRICKS

Painting a brick wall is another easy, enjoyable project. It's really just a matter of stamping paint onto *dry* fabric with a plain old household sponge. Imagine the possibilities of a brick wall as a support for some lovely vines, the side of a building, or a foreground that makes the viewer feel like a voyeur, peeking at distant meadows and hills.

Supplies

See Tools and Equipment for Painting Fabric (pages 11-18) for information on paint and supplies.

- Copper metallic opaque paint
- Silver metallic opaque paint
- Gray transparent paint
- Black transparent paint
- 2 or 3 brushes
- 2 rectangular household sponges
- Containers for mixing paints
- Previously painted or commercial fabric

Mixing Paints

Refer to Mixing Colors (pages 14-16) for information on mixing paints.

1. Add just enough water to allow the paints to flow easily.

2. Swirl a couple of colors in a mixing container without completely mixing them together. This will give a more random, mottled look to the bricks. Start with a copper and black combination.

3. Test the colors on a dry test cloth.

Painting Bricks

I like to paint bricks on a neutral-colored dry fabric. Gray is my favorite background because it blends nicely with the brick colors and fills in the little holes created by the sponge.

> **TIP**
>
> *Before painting, draw a few straight guidelines for the rows of bricks. I didn't do that the first time I tried painting bricks, and my wall betrayed me as a very inept mason!*

1. Brush a copper and black combination onto one of the sponges. Brushing the paint onto the sponge, rather than dipping the sponge into the paint, gives you more control over how much paint adheres to the sponge.

2. Press the sponge onto the fabric. Don't worry if you don't get a complete image. Irregularity in the bricks creates far more interest—and, anyway, you will be adding other layers of color.

3. Repeat Step 1 with the second sponge, using a gray and silver combination.

4. Press this color over the copper images, as well as on other areas of your brick wall.

Note: If you add too much gray-silver to a brick, you can simply go over that with another pressing of copper.

5. To add mortar to the bricks, mix a gray and silver combination. Lightly dab this between the bricks. Keep a light hand with the mortar so the bricks will retain a rough-edged look.

ROCKS

A few rocks strategically placed in a foreground can add another interesting element to your artwork. At first, these will take a bit of practice, so play around with the technique until you feel comfortable adding it after your painted foreground has completely dried.

Supplies

See Tools and Equipment for Painting Fabric (pages 11-18) for information on paint and supplies.

- Black transparent paint
- Gray transparent paint
- Gray-violet transparent paint
- Pearl metallic opaque paint (optional)
- 2 or 3 foam brushes
- Small detail brush
- Containers for mixing paints
- Previously painted fabric

Mixing Paints

Refer to Mixing Colors (pages 14-16) for information on mixing paints.

1. Add just enough water to allow the paints to flow easily.

2. Mix some transparent colors into the opaque metallics. I find that the opacity of the metallics gives me the covering I need, and the transparent paints keep the finished rocks from becoming stiff or gummy.

3. Test the colors on a dry test cloth.

Painting Rocks

Note: Using a foam brush provides you with more control over the shapes.

1. Begin by painting a few gray rock shapes on dry fabric.

2. Add some gray-violet shapes to build up each rock.

3. While the rocks are still wet, anchor them into the landscape by using a small detail brush to streak a bit of black paint at the base of each rock. Add some skinny streaks on a couple of rocks for texture.

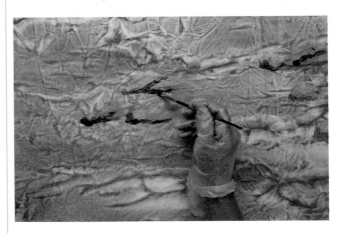

4. Keep adding rocks until you're happy with the result.

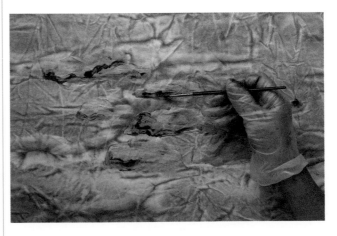

STONE WALL

If you like puzzles and have a bit of patience, the following method for painting a stone wall can be fun, and the results are worth every minute.

Supplies

See Tools and Equipment for Painting Fabric (pages 11–18) for information on paint and supplies.

- Black transparent paint
- Gray transparent paint
- Brown transparent paint
- Pearl metallic opaque paint
- Copper metallic opaque paint
- 2 or 3 brushes
- Brayer
- 1–2 sheets of Miracle Sponge (Resources, page 94)
- Several 8½˝ × 11˝ sheets of self-adhesive label paper
- Scissors
- Containers for mixing paints
- Previously painted dry fabric

Mixing Paints

Refer to Mixing Colors (pages 14-16) for information on mixing paints.

1. Add just enough water to allow the paints to flow easily.

2. Mix some opaque metallic paint into each transparent paint: some copper into the brown, pearl into the black and gray. Again, the opacity of the metallics will cover colors and shapes that may exist on the fabric.

3. Test the colors on a dry test cloth.

Painting a Stone Wall

1. Before mixing your paints, cut 1 or 2 sheets of Miracle Sponge into random interlocking shapes. (You might like the security of drawing the lines on paper first just to get the idea.) As you cut the shapes, place each one in order on a piece of sticky-backed label paper to keep track of positioning.

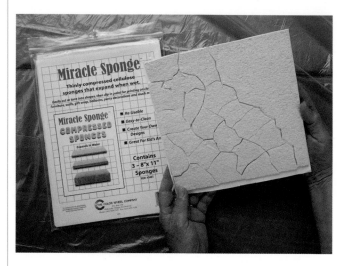

2. After the paints are mixed and everything is ready to go, lightly spray the sponge pieces until they are damp enough to expand.

3. Lift the first sponge shape off the paper, turn it over, and paint the back with a brush.

4. Place the painted side down on your fabric and press lightly.

5. Roll a brayer over the piece to apply even pressure, ensuring that the paint will print.

6. Replace the sponge piece on the paper to keep the shapes in order. Pick up the adjacent piece.

7. Continue picking up, painting, printing, and replacing the sponge shapes, varying the paint colors.

8. Keep building your wall in this manner until it's as tall and as long as you wish.

Note: Because this is just a fantasy wall, you won't have to worry about it falling down if your shapes get a bit out of order. Simply fit them in as you go along, perhaps adding a lone rock here and there.

9. Paint a bit of diluted gray to the base of the wall to anchor the stones in place.

What a wonderful focal point a stone wall would be in your quilt!

WOOD GRAIN

How about adding a rail fence, tree trunks, an old barn, or cabin in the woods to your next SkyQuilt? Here's an easy method to paint the texture of wood.

Supplies

See Tools and Equipment for Painting Fabric (page 11) for information on paint and supplies.

- Brown transparent paint

- Brown-black transparent paint

- Gold metallic opaque paint

- 2 natural sponges

- 2 containers for mixing paints, large enough to accommodate sponges

- Previously painted dry fabric

Mixing Paints

Refer to Mixing Colors (pages 14–16) for information on mixing paints.

1. Add just enough water to allow the paints to flow easily. Be sure not to add too much water, or the paint will bleed and flow too much to retain defined lines in the wood.

2. Mix some gold metallic into the brown paint to give a little sparkle to the finished piece.

3. Test the colors on a dry test cloth.

Painting Wood Grain

Note: I like to paint wood grain on a dry piece of light brown painted fabric. I allow this light brown color to show through in a few areas to create more texture in the grain.

1. Dip the edge of a sponge in one of your colors.

2. Drag this color lightly across your fabric.

3. Alternate colors and continue until you are happy with the effect. But don't overdo it, or you will lose the lovely grainlines.

 By this time you should have a good stash of your own painted fabrics that are just crying out to become quilts.

SKYQUILT PROJECTS
USING THE DESIGN STRIP METHOD

The wonderful feature of a SkyQuilt is that it uses a wholecloth sky and a wholecloth foreground—no angst and stress from the fear of cutting up those favorites!

So it's time to put all those beautiful painted fabrics to work.

The first step is to decide whether you prefer piecing, appliquéing, or fusing. The design strip for *Mountains* (page 50) can be pieced, appliquéd, or fused fairly easily. However, for *Beach Houses* (page 55), piecing or fusing is suggested because of all the sharp angles.

For something small and quick, I've included one additional project, *City Pillow* (page 62), designed for stenciling or fusing.

The following projects are intended to get you started, and I'm sure that many of you will want to design your own projects when you see how easy it is.

After you have decided on a project, choose a sky and foreground. These first two fabrics will determine the colors of the pieces in the design strip (page 10). Hang the sky and foreground on a wall and stand back. Do the sky and foreground look as though they both belong at the same time of day (morning, afternoon, or night)? Is there at least one unifying color in both pieces? Do they complement each other? Perhaps you just love the sky fabric; if that's the case, make the sky fabric the star of the quilt and give the foreground fabric a supporting role, or vice versa. The composition of your quilt will be more visually appealing if the sky takes up approximately one- or two-thirds of the finished piece. You may wish to pair a quiet horizontal sky with a textured foreground for more interest and contrast. Or, to convey a peaceful mood, you might choose a sky and foreground both painted with horizontal strokes.

TIP

To get different views, try looking at the reflection of pairs of fabric in a mirror or take a quick digital photo. Both of these perspectives help me see my fabric choices in a new way.

TOOLS YOU WILL NEED

Basic drafting and sewing supplies are all you will need for the projects in this chapter.

- Sharp pencils
- Graph paper
- Template plastic
- Craft knife, such as an X-Acto knife
- Cutting board
- Stencil plastic or Mylar polyester film
- Stencil brush
- Ruler
- Paper-backed fusible web
- Rotary cutter and mat
- Scissors
- Permanent pen
- Temporary marker
- Hand-sewing needles
- Thread
- Straight pins
- Sewing machine (optional)

MOUNTAINS

Mountains, by Mickey Lawler, 36" × 36", 2010

This quilt began on a lovely spring morning with a kitchen table, a cup of coffee, a pencil, and a few doodles.

The drawing sat in a file for a year or so until I found I was to be away from home for a few days without a sewing machine. I decided to use graph paper to transpose it into a pieced design. I quickly cut out all the pieces; gathered some needles, pins, and thread; and had the whole project in a baggie, ready to be hand-pieced during those few quiet evenings in my daughter Mary's small apartment.

View of Hip Mountain, by Mickey Lawler, 37″ × 33″, 2007

This is the pieced version of *Mountains*. A full-sized pattern is located on the pullout (page P-1). Refer to Piecing *Beach Houses* (pages 56-60) for general piecing instructions.

As time went by, the mountain shapes cried out to be gentler, more rounded, like the original sketch, and to be appliquéd. The beauty of an appliqué design like the one on page 50 is that the shapes are irregular, so following the outlines accurately isn't crucial. Though I have very little rest and recreation time, I do enjoy the rare moments when I can sit, relax, and hand stitch an appliqué piece. The pattern also works well for machine appliqué, raw-edge appliqué, or fusing—whichever you like best.

CHOOSING THE FABRIC

For *Mountains,* I wanted to use a beautiful piece of foreground fabric that I had painted. Obviously, the foreground would have a starring role in this quilt, so I assigned it about two-thirds of the finished piece. I then tried out a few skies before settling on a warm evening sky that enhanced some of the foreground colors. Because I was doing hand appliqué, I cut a 5″-wide strip from the sky fabric to reserve as a background for my appliquéd mountains.

I auditioned several painted scraps before deciding on some purple pieces that I had painted using the scrunch method (page 39) and one or two that were part of larger sky pieces. Purple was a nice complement to the yellow-orange sky. I paid particular attention to contrasting values—light, medium, and dark—to make sure my mountains conveyed a sense of varied distances. I also chose fabrics that had lines and shadowlike textures.

Supplies

- Sky fabric, at least 36″ × 22″

- Foreground fabric, at least 36″ × 22″

- Painted fabric scraps for mountain appliqués

- Template plastic

- Permanent pen

- Gluestick

- 2 pairs of scissors (for plastic and for fabric)

- Removable marker (optional)

- Thread

- Straight pins

- Hand-sewing needle (optional)

- Sewing machine

HAND APPLIQUÉ FOR MOUNTAINS

Preparing the Pieces

1. Cut a 5″-wide strip from the sky fabric to use as a background for the appliquéd mountains. You could appliqué the mountains directly to the entire sky fabric, but I prefer to work on a smaller, more manageable piece. I also like having the option of attaching the finished design strip to a different sky piece if the spirit moves me.

2. Trace all pattern pieces (Pattern Pullout P-1) onto template plastic with a permanent pen, marking each piece with the corresponding letter and making a slash where each mountain intersects with another. Cut each plastic template on the drawn lines.

Trace pattern onto template plastic.

Note: See Fusing *Mountains* (page 54) for instructions on fusing this quilt.

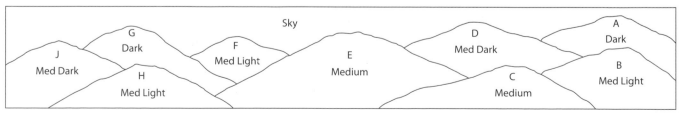

Fabric placement for *Mountains* appliqué design strip

3. Use a permanent pen or pencil to draw around each template on the *right* side of the fabric. If you prefer to use a temporary or removable marker, follow the manufacturer's directions carefully.

4. Cut the fabric pieces approximately ½˝ outside the drawn sewing line. This ½˝ will allow you to move the mountains around a bit without worrying about them not overlapping. In addition, as you appliqué, you can cut the needle-turned edges down to ⅛˝ or so.

> **TIP**
>
> *One of the benefits of using a more tightly woven fabric such as broadcloth is that edges won't fray with scant ⅛˝ seam allowances.*

5. Audition your fabrics again and make any changes, perhaps cutting some other pieces to see which ones work best.

6. When all the fabric pieces are marked and cut, place them on the sky strip and take a critical look at the combination.

7. When you're satisfied with the arrangement, fine-tune the placement of each mountain by lining up the slash marks with the adjacent pieces.

8. Put a dab of glue on the back of each piece to hold the pieces in place. I prefer using a gluestick on painted fabric, because pins often leave pinhole marks.

Hand Appliquéing

I prefer to use a strong, fine thread, like Bottom Line by Superior Threads, and size 12 between needles, though sharps have bigger eyes and may be more user friendly. Bottom Line thread gives me no trouble getting through the small eye of a between. Everyone has a preference, so just choose the appliqué style with which you're most comfortable.

1. Appliqué the most distant mountain first (the one behind all the others); then work forward, layer by layer, to the closest mountain, which will cover parts of the previous mountains.

2. With your needle or fingernail, turn under the raw edges hiding the line you drew and stitch as you go.

3. Continue to work across the strip in this fashion, moving or adjusting mountain pieces if needed.

Putting the Quilt Together

1. Place the design strip on the wall with the sky and foreground fabric. Take another look at the combination. Move the sky and foreground fabrics up and down to select the best placement.

2. When you are pleased with the placement, cut the sky and the foreground, leaving a ¼˝ seam allowance on all sides.

3. Pin and stitch the sky and foreground to the design strip, using a ¼˝ seam allowance. I press seams open when I want a smooth transition between the 3 elements. On the other hand, I often press the lower seam allowance toward the foreground to give the design strip the appearance of being farther in the distance.

4. Trim the edges of your finished quilt top to square it up.

5. Refer to Borders and Finishing (pages 66-68) to finish the quilt.

FUSING MOUNTAINS

TIP

You can make your mountains larger or smaller by enlarging or reducing your design strip pattern.

Preparing the Design Strip Background for Fusing

Cut a strip of sky fabric for the design strip background. Make certain to add ½˝ to both the desired height and width measurements of the design strip to allow for a ¼˝ seam allowance on each side.

Preparing the Pieces

1. Choose the mountain fabrics.

2. Trace the mountain pattern pieces (Pattern Pullout P-1) in reverse on the paper side of paper-backed fusible web. *Note:* You do not need to cut out the sky pieces for the fused version.

3. Iron the fusible web to the wrong side of the selected fabrics. Cut out the pieces, allowing some extra on the sides for overlap.

4. Audition your fabrics on the background and make any changes, perhaps cutting some additional pieces to see which ones work best.

5. Pin or use glue to tack the pieces in place. Or iron directly on your design wall if it can handle the heat of an iron.

6. You may wish to stitch the mountains in place along the raw edges after fusing.

TIP

If you use Steam-A-Seam 2 fusible web, it has a pressure-sensitive temporary adhesive side that allows you to position and reposition your pieces. You can then leave them in place while you move your quilt top to the ironing surface to permanently fuse.

Completing the Quilt Top

1. Place the background on an ironing surface and fuse the mountains in place according to the manufacturer's instructions. Remove any pins before ironing.

2. Place the design strip on the wall with the sky and foreground fabric so you can take another look at the combination. Move the sky and foreground fabrics up and down to select the best placement. When you are pleased with the placement, cut the sky and the foreground, leaving a ¼˝ seam allowance.

3. Pin and stitch the sky and foreground to the design strip, using a ¼˝ seam allowance. I press seams open when I want a smooth transition between the 3 elements. On the other hand, I often press the lower seam allowance toward the foreground to give the design strip the appearance of being farther in the distance.

4. Trim the edges of your finished quilt top to square it up.

5. Refer to Borders and Finishing (pages 66–68) to finish the quilt.

BEACH HOUSES

Beach Houses 3, by Mickey Lawler, 37″ × 37″, 2010

Because I enjoy the geometrics and process of piecing a quilt, I designed *Beach Houses 3* to be pieced. But you can fuse your project if you choose.

I have three houses on my beach; however, you may have as many or as few as you wish.

CHOOSING THE FABRICS

The first decision will be whether you intend your houses to be in the distance (far away from the viewer) or closer to the viewer near the foreground. This decision is often determined by whether you want your quilt to show more sky fabric or more foreground fabric.

After auditioning several colors, I decided on orange tones for my houses, so they would draw the viewer into the distance and not be overpowered by the strong foreground.

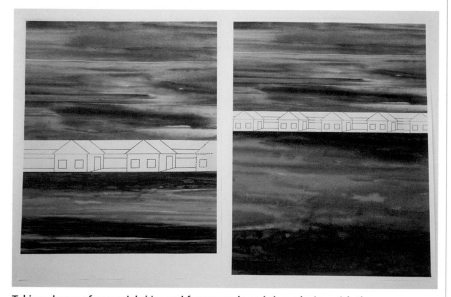

Taking photos of potential skies and foregrounds and then playing with the arrangements in a photo-editing program, such as Adobe Photoshop, is a quick way to make design decisions. You can also just print out the photos and cut and paste until you like the arrangement. Consider coloring in the houses with colored pencils or watercolors to help you make fabric selections.

To give perspective and dimension to the houses, choose three different values of the house fabric. Because my scene is a sunny day, the roof fabric will be the lightest color, the right-hand side of the house will be a bit darker, and the front of the house the darkest. Allow yourself to be flexible. Once you have cut the pieces, audition them again before making a final decision. Sometimes a piece just doesn't work, and you may have to cut another. I often have several rejects at the end of a project.

Build up a good stash of scraps and trial pieces to use for design elements, such as the houses. These can be small left-over pieces of painted fabric or fabric you have intentionally painted for this design.

You may have a favorite method for tracing, cutting, and piecing a quilt. In that case, just do what works best for you. Because I really hate to rip out stitches, I've always liked the security and accuracy of seeing my sewing lines when I piece. If you want to try my method, follow the steps in this section.

Supplies

- Painted sky fabric, at least 36″ × 22″

- Painted foreground fabric, at least 36″ × 22″

- Painted water fabric, approximately 36″ × 4″

- Painted fabric scraps for beach houses

- Template plastic for piecing

- Permanent pen for drawing on template plastic

- Pencil for tracing templates on fabric

- 2 pairs of scissors (for plastic and for fabric)

- Paper-backed fusible web for windows and doors

PIECING BEACH HOUSES

Preparing the Pieces

1. Because you will need to include a small amount of the sky and foreground fabrics in the design strip, cut a 3″–4″-wide strip from the *bottom* of the sky and another from the *top* of the foreground before you begin. These will be used as background in the design strip. Set aside for now. This enables the sky and foreground to flow into the middle of the design strip. The K piece will also be cut from this reserved fabric. The H and J pieces will be added later.

2. Trace all pattern pieces (Pattern Pullout P-2) on template plastic with a permanent pen, marking each piece with the letter. Cut each template accurately.

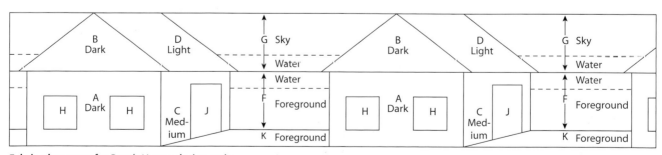

Fabric placement for *Beach Houses* **design strip**

Note: See Fusing *Beach Houses* (page 61) for instructions on fusing this quilt.

3. Decide how many houses you want on the beach. Use the templates to draw the appropriate number of the A, B, C, and D pattern pieces onto the wrong side of the fabric. The lines on the fabric will be the sewing lines. Because some of the pattern pieces have a specific direction to them, be sure to turn templates C, D, J, and K to the wrong side when tracing them onto the fabric. I use a pencil to trace on the fabric whenever possible. However, sometimes it's difficult to see a pencil line; so I use a permanent marker instead. Other people prefer a removable marker. Use whatever suits you.

4. Cut the fabric pieces approximately ¼″ outside the drawn sewing line.

5. Audition your fabrics again and make any changes, perhaps cutting some additional pieces to see which work best.

6. To save time and ensure more accuracy for the F and G pieces, first cut 2 strips of water fabric approximately 36″ × 1″. Then, on the wrong side of the fabric, trace a sewing line ¼″ in from the edges.

7. For the K pieces, take the reserved strip of foreground fabric from Step 1, and cut a long strip approximately 36″ × 1″. On the wrong side of the fabric, trace a sewing line ¼″ in from the edges. Reverse the K template before tracing on the wrong side of the fabric.

8. Take your reserved strip of sky fabric from Step 1, and cut a long strip 1¾″ wide. Draw a sewing line ¼″ in from the edges on the wrong side of the fabric. Do the same for the reserved strip of foreground fabric.

9. With right sides together, pin the sky strip to a water strip, matching the sewing lines. Sew these 2 strips together to form the unit from which the G pieces will be cut.

10. With right sides together, pin the 1¾″ foreground strip to a water strip, matching the sewing lines. Sew these 2 strips together to form the unit from which the F pieces will be cut.

You now have 3 strips from which to cut the F, G, and K pieces.

— Water
— Foreground
— Sky
— Water
— Foreground

11. Place the F template on the wrong side of the foreground/water strip, aligning the seamline drawn on the template with the seam of the sewn strip. Draw around the template. Repeat to make two F pieces to insert between the houses. Reserve the remainder of this strip to fill in the sides of the design strip.

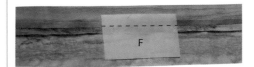

Place F template on wrong side of water/foreground strip.

12. Repeat Step 11 for the G pieces on the sky/water strip.

13. Draw around the K template on the single foreground strip. Cut out the pieces about ¼″ outside the sewing lines.

14. Draw around the H and J templates on the paper side of the fusible web. Place the fusible web on the wrong side of scrap fabric. Cut **on** the sewing line and fuse each piece in place on pieces A and C. Because they are fused, windows and doors can be added at any time.

Piecing

When I design a pieced quilt, I'm always aware of the piecing sequence. I try to make my life easier by breaking the pattern into simple units whenever possible. *Beach Houses 3* has two major units in the design strip. The top portion consists of the roofs (B and D) joined to G. The bottom portion of the design strip consists of the walls of the house (A and C) joined to F, and finally to K, which was the only place where I had to sew into a corner.

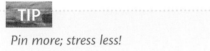

TIP

Pin more; stress less!

1. For the roof unit, match the drawn sewing lines of the B pieces to the D pieces and pin often. Sew the B's to the D's on the sewing line. Sew the left side of G to D and the right side of G to B of the next unit until you have the number of houses you want for your quilt.

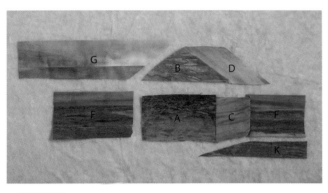

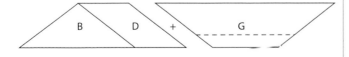

Design strip roof assembly

2. For the wall unit, match the drawn sewing lines of the A pieces to the C pieces and pin often. Sew the A's to the C's on the sewing line. Sew the left side of F to C, making sure to stop and backstitch at the end of the drawn line (¼˝ from the bottom edge), so you can later sew K into that corner. Don't sew the right side of F to A of the next unit until you have added the K piece (Step 3).

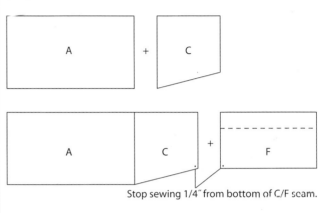

Stop sewing 1/4˝ from bottom of C/F seam.

3. Carefully pin and sew the K piece by first stitching the top of K to F, stopping at the C/F seam. Turn the piece and stitch the angled side of K to the angled side of C.

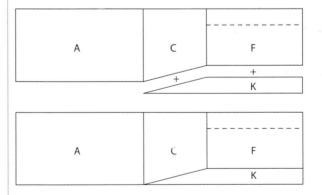

TIP

To make sure you don't get a ripple when sewing into corners, stop sewing a stitch or two before the end of the line.

4. To isolate just a few houses on the landscape, as I did, use the G template at either end of the design strip to cut long left and right pieces from the remaining G strip. Do this for the F and K pieces as well.

The G, F, and K pieces at the left and right sides of the design strip can be lengthened to fit the width of your quilt.

5. Line up the roof strip with the wall strip, pin well, and sew the 2 strips together. Your design strip is done!

TIP

I often machine baste the wall unit strip and the roof unit strip together first to make sure they are positioned the way I want them.

Putting the Quilt Together

1. Place the design strip on the wall with the sky and foreground fabric. Take another look at the combination. Move the sky and foreground fabrics up and down to select the best placement.

2. When you are pleased with the placement, draw a sewing line on the wrong side of both the sky and the foreground pieces. Cut the sky and the foreground about ¼˝ outside the drawn lines.

3. Pin and stitch the sky and foreground to the design strip, matching sewing lines on the design strip to the sewing lines on the sky and the foreground.

4. Trim the edges of your finished quilt top to square it up.

5. Refer to Borders and Finishing (pages 66–68) to finish the quilt.

Analyzing Your Quilt

When you have all the pieces of your quilt on the design wall, take a good look. Do the colors at the top of the design strip flow into the colors at the bottom of the sky? For example, you may have a bit of blue on the left side of the design strip sky.

Does it meet some blue on the left side of the sky piece? Paying attention to placement provides a seamless flow to the composition.

In the project quilt (page 55), the blue on the left side of the design strip sky flows into the blue on the left side of the sky fabric.

FUSING BEACH HOUSES

Fusing is a speedy alternative to needle-turn appliqué and is entirely suitable for SkyQuilts. Remember to reverse the templates before tracing on the fusible web; otherwise, the appliqués will be a mirror image of the patterns!

Preparing the Design Strip for Fusing

1. Cut a strip of water fabric about 1½″ × 22″.

2. Assemble the design strip background using a ¼″ seam allowance to sew the sky, water, and foreground fabrics together, with the water in the center.

3. Press the seams.

Preparing the Pieces

1. Trace pattern pieces A, B, C, D, H, and J for the houses (Pattern Pullout P-2) *in reverse* on the paper side of paper-backed fusible web. **Note:** You do not need to cut out the sky, water, or foreground pieces in the design strip.

2. Iron the fusible web to the wrong side of the selected fabrics. Cut out the fabric pieces on the drawn line.

3. Audition your fabric pieces on the background and make any changes, perhaps cutting additional pieces to see which work best. Try different placements of the houses on the background.

4. Pin or use glue to tack the pieces in place. Or iron directly on your design wall if it can handle the heat of an iron.

TIP

If you use Steam-A-Seam 2 fusible web, it has a pressure-sensitive temporary adhesive that allows you to position and reposition your pieces. You can then leave them in place while you move your quilt top to the ironing surface to permanently fuse.

Completing the Quilt Top

1. Place the background on an ironing surface and fuse the houses in place according to the manufacturer's instructions. Remove any pins before ironing.

2. Place the design strip on the wall with the sky and foreground fabric so you can take another look at the combination. Move the sky and foreground fabrics up and down to select the best placement.

3. Pin and stitch the sky and foreground to the design strip using any sewing lines you've drawn.

4. Trim the edges of your finished quilt top to square it up.

5. Refer to Borders and Finishing (pages 66–68) to finish the quilt.

CITY PILLOW

City Pillow 2, by Mickey Lawler, 16″ × 16″, 2010

In 1998, my daughter Terry had to make a quick gift for a friend in New York. She wanted to do a small quilt but found herself very short on time. That's when she came up with the idea of stenciling a cityscape onto a piece of black fabric that she had spattered with paint. She added a painted moon to the scene, then dipped her fingernails in gold paint and quickly dabbed on the "windows." Finally she quilted it, bound it, sewed on a sleeve, and, presto, a wonderful gift for a wonderful friend.

Terry's quilt was the inspiration for my own City stencil design. I decided to make the stencil in several sections so that I could move the sections around on the fabric, allowing me more freedom for each new city.

The City stencil design (Pattern Pullout P-2) is so simple that you may want to copy it for fusing, appliquéing, or even transposing onto graph paper for a pieced quilt. Consider scanning it into photo-editing software and enlarging the sections for a wall quilt.

CHOOSING THE FABRIC

I love doing this project in the design strip method. If I make a mistake, I can simply start over again on a new strip of fabric, knowing I haven't ruined a valuable sky or foreground piece. Because the sky or foreground parts of my design strip can flow into many different sky and foreground pieces of similar colors when I'm finished, I don't have to worry about making every-thing match at the start of my project. Half the fun of this project is knowing you can change your mind with little stress!

MAKING CITY PILLOW

For my pillow, I cut a piece from a rather plain painted fabric for the design strip background. I had a blue sky fabric with a touch of yellow in mind and a soft multicolor foreground, but I knew that I could play around with other skies and foregrounds with yellows as well. Also, because the finished project was going to be so small, I didn't need to commit a big piece to complete the scene.

Supplies

- 3 painted fabric pieces 7″ × 18″ for design strip, foreground, and sky (Fabric size will depend on the size of your pillow form.)
- Stencil plastic or Mylar polyester film
- Craft knife, such as an X-Acto knife
- Cutting mat
- Opaque and metallic paints—undiluted
- Stencil brushes
- Artist's tape
- 16″ × 16″ pillow form

Tracing and Cutting the Stencil

1. Copy the original pattern (Pullout P-2) onto another piece of paper.

2. Use artist's tape to secure the stencil plastic onto the paper copy and then onto the cutting mat. Artist's tape can be removed easily from the paper and the plastic without tearing either.

3. On your cutting mat, cut the stencil with a craft knife to ensure control and accuracy. Use a bit of pressure, so that you don't have to go back over the lines. A ruler may be helpful to guide the knife.

4. Consider saving the plastic buildings that you have cut to use as templates for a later fused design (page 65).

5. Tape the stencil on the design strip fabric on a painting surface.

6. Load the stencil brush with paint, then dab off excess paint on a paper towel. You will be working with what is known as a dry brush, using just the barest amount of paint. Practice on a test fabric if this is a new technique for you.

7. Holding the brush perpendicular to the stencil, dab the paint on the stencil until the shape is completely painted.

8. Continue to stencil all the buildings, changing colors as desired.

TIP

Use a small, stiff brush for the skinny buildings.

9. When you are finished, allow the paint to dry in place and clean the stencil.

Note: I added a second layer of buildings to make the city more complex and to give it some perspective. Because you are working with opaque paints, you can easily cover the original paint. Choose where you would like to add buildings and move the stencil over those areas. Paint as previously and allow the piece to dry in place.

Finishing the Pillow

1. Audition the finished stenciled strip with sky and foreground pieces and make any changes before sewing. Decide on the proportion of sky and foreground.

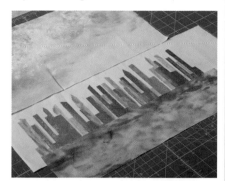

After I had the entire design stenciled, I auditioned several choices for the sky to decide which I liked best. The advantage of the separate strip!

2. Sew the sky and foreground to the stenciled strip. Trim the pillow top to the preferred size. If desired, add borders to the pillow front.

3. Layer the pillow front with batting and quilt as desired (page 68).

4. With right sides together, sew a back fabric onto the pillow top, leaving an opening on one side for inserting the pillow form. Turn right side out and press.

5. Insert the pillow form and hand stitch the opening closed.

City Pillow 1, by Mickey Lawler, 16″ x16″, 2010. This is a dark, stormy version of the project.

Fusing the City Pillow

Note: If you have traced and cut the City stencil, you can use the cutouts as patterns for fusing. If not, create templates from the City Pillow design strip template pattern (Pullout P-2).

1. Trace the building cutouts onto the paper side of fusible web.

2. Following the steps for fusing *Mountains* (page 54), cut and place the fabric pieces onto a design strip background; fuse. Stitch the pieces in place.

3. Follow Steps 1–5 of Finishing the Pillow (above) to complete the project.

BORDERS AND FINISHING

BORDERS

Some quilts need a frame, or border, to set off the design, enclose the quilt, or provide a finished look. I generally try to choose a border that repeats some color in the quilt. If the fabrics in the quilt are all hand painted, I often stay in that style and choose a hand-painted fabric for the border. Most of the time, I just audition different fabrics for a border. The borders on *Beach Houses 2* and *View of Hip Mountain* were both cut from dark painted fabric to repeat the mood of the quilts.

View of Hip Mountain, by Mickey Lawler, 37″ × 33″, 2007

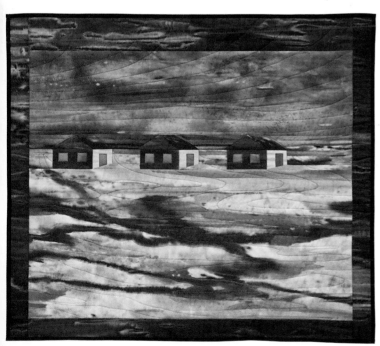

Beach Houses 2, by Mickey Lawler, 37″ × 33″, 2007

A border isn't always necessary. If it doesn't add to the visual impact of the quilt, you may simply wish to add a binding to the quilt.

A binding worked well for my *Tile Triptych* (larger image on page 85), where borders would have interrupted the three designs.

There are so many methods for adding borders and binding that I suggest you choose your favorite.

BACKING AND LAYERING

For the backing, you may want to paint a specific piece of fabric to go with the quilt top. Or you can sew together several leftover pieces of painted fabric.

When you have made or selected the backing, layer the quilt top, batting, and backing fabric. Pin or thread baste the layers together.

QUILTING

I believe that quilting should enhance your SkyQuilt and not become the focus of the quilt. After all, you have taken a good deal of time to paint and select the fabric for your quilt. This is your artistry. You want to make the quilting embellish your work.

I sometimes follow the patterns of the paint. Other times, I like to add lines that reinforce the sense of a gentle sky, a foreground moving into the distance, or texture in the mountains.

Detail of *Mountains* (page 50)

Detail of *Beach Houses* 3 (page 55)

My favorite way to design the quilting is to print a large photo of my finished quilt top.

Then I place tracing paper over the photo and draw quilting lines with a pencil to see the effect. I keep replacing the tracing paper and redrawing quilting lines until I am satisfied with one.

Use tracing paper to audition quilting designs.

I then loosely transfer those lines freehand onto my quilt top with a hard pencil or water-soluble marker. This can be a little tricky, so draw very lightly the first time.

Hooray! Now just hand or machine quilt, bind the quilt, and your SkyQuilt is finished.

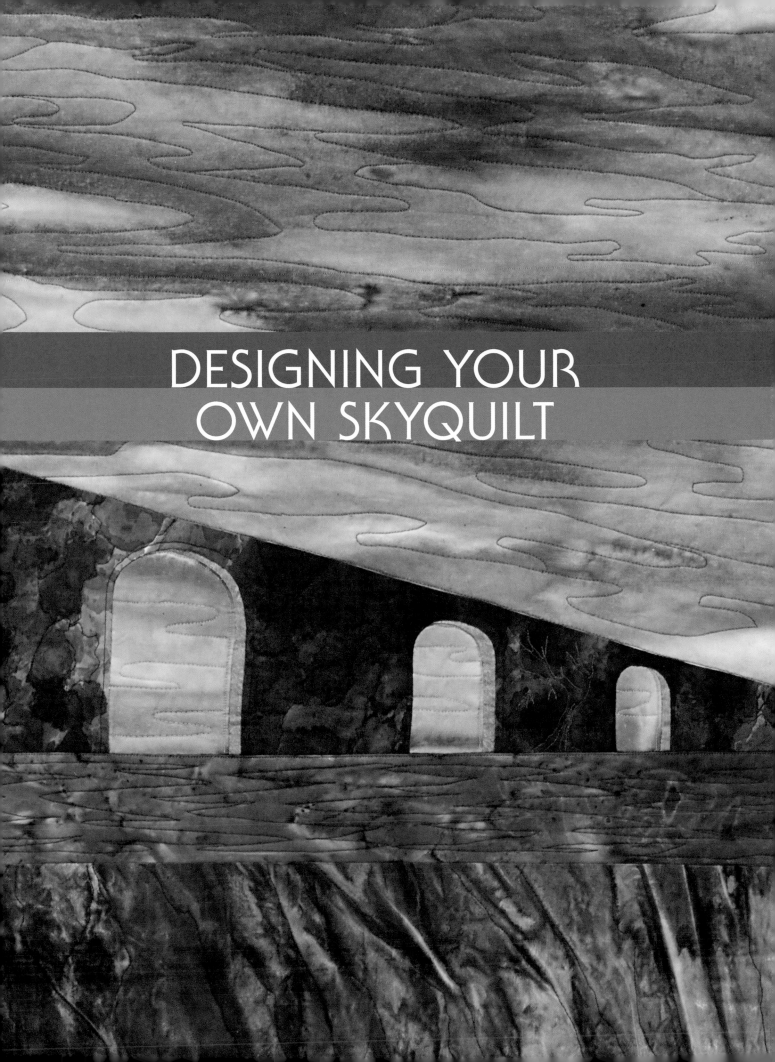

DESIGNING YOUR OWN SKYQUILT

Starting a new design is one of the most exciting times for any quilt project. It's that moment when an idea pops into your head and you think, "That would make a great quilt!" It's the rush of adrenaline as you find renewed inspiration—the preparation stage of the creative process.

However, you soon come down to earth because the next stage of the creative process can be stressful. This is when the steps to completing your vision become ambiguous, when many questions arise—"What do I do next? Where do I start? How can I turn my idea into a quilt?"

The third stage requires patience so the idea can simmer in your mind. During this period, as you go about your daily routine, your brain is working on problem solving. Give it a little time; draw a few doodles. Have faith that your subconscious is not going to let you down.

Then, happily, at some point, you arrive at the *ah-ha* phase. Lightbulbs go on, frowns go away, and joy reigns once again in your creative heart.

Now the work begins.

DRAWING THE DESIGN

After you understand the concept of the design strip quilt (page 10), it's an easy next step to creating your own designs. Here's the general process that I follow.

1. When I begin a new SkyQuilt design, I like to draw a few lines on a sketchpad. However, to be honest, I often just grab the nearest piece of paper or the back of an envelope when an idea strikes. (I have to quickly tack my drawing on a bulletin board so it doesn't get tossed into the recycling bin.)

2. I then usually draw the design on graph paper. This helps me see how I can make the design work as a pieced quilt. I do this for appliqué designs as well, because I can easily enlarge the design later.

3. From my large pad of graph paper, I cut a strip of paper a little bigger than the size I want my finished design strip to be. If I am planning a large quilt, I tape a couple of pieces together.

4. I draw (and often redraw) the design on the full-sized strip of paper. When I'm pleased with the design, I trace over the pencil lines with a black permanent pen so they will be easy to see if I decide to make plastic templates.

VARIATIONS USING PERSPECTIVE

The design strip for your SkyQuilt doesn't always have to be a rectangle. By angling the strip, you can achieve a different perspective.

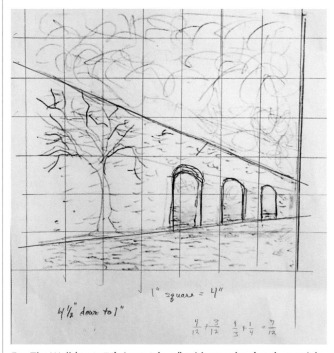

For *The Wall* (page 71), I traced a 1˝ grid over the sketch, a quick alternative to copying the design onto graph paper. I then drew the full-size pattern for this quilt on a large piece of graph paper.

The Wall, by Mickey Lawler, 31″ × 32″, 2010

This perspective makes viewers feel as if they are looking up at the wall from the left. I added a rich scrunch piece to the bottom of this quilt as another foreground element.

Any design strips, including those for *Beach Houses* (page 55) and *Mountains* (page 50), can be drawn at an angle using a *vanishing point* to provide a different perspective. If you are unsure about, or unfamiliar with, drawing perspective, check out your local bookstore, go online, or visit the library to learn more about it. Once you get the hang of perspective, designing your quilts will take on a whole new dimension.

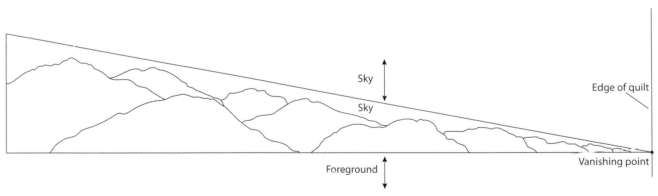

Design strip using perspective with the vanishing point *inside* **the frame**

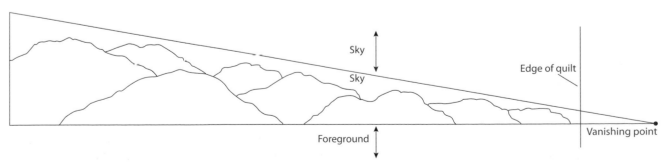

Design strip using perspective with the vanishing point *outside* **the frame**

DESIGNING FROM A PHOTOGRAPH OR ILLUSTRATION

Adobe Photoshop Elements is a user-friendly computer program that you can use to copy and enlarge, as well as enhance and alter, photographs or illustrations.

If you don't want to use a computer, follow these steps to turn your photo or drawing into a SkyQuilt design strip:

1. Enlarge the photo or drawing to at least 8″ × 10″ to make it a workable size.

2. Draw a grid onto the enlarged copy.

3. Simplify the design by drawing a new one onto graph paper or a paper strip with a grid corresponding to the original.

USING A COMPUTER QUILT DESIGN PROGRAM

For those who enjoy and appreciate its benefits, the computer is terrific for designing. The Electric Quilt Company (see Resources, page 94) has been writing excellent design programs for quilters since the early years of the personal computer. Their program EQ7 is another wonderful tool for designing your SkyQuilt.

You now have all the tools you need to design your own quilt, free from the stress of cutting into beautiful one-of-a-kind hand-painted fabrics. The first Gallery (page 73) offers a wonderful variety of SkyQuilts made with painted fabric.

In addition, you undoubtedly have several trial pieces left over from practicing your painting or from your stash. In the second Gallery (page 84), you will see how some scraps and rejected pieces were transformed into beautiful quilts.

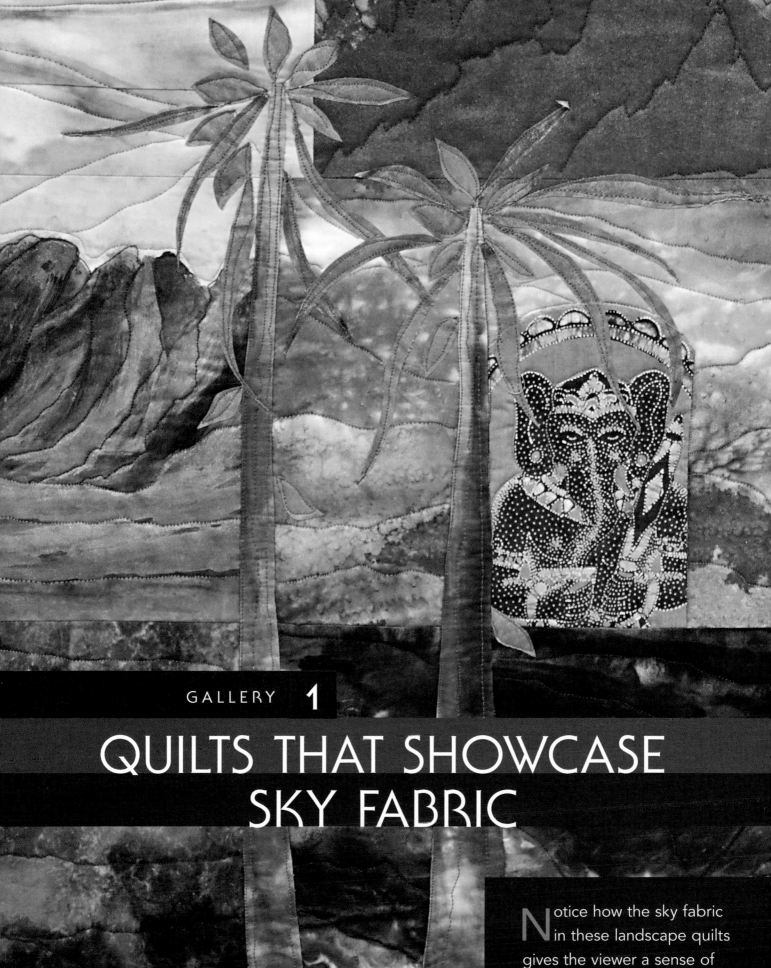

QUILTS THAT SHOWCASE SKY FABRIC

Notice how the sky fabric in these landscape quilts gives the viewer a sense of place and controls the mood of the scene.

Tim's Quilt,
by Mickey Lawler,
38″ × 46″, 2008

■ Made for Tim Mayes, a young neighbor who has been my right-hand man through blizzards, broken tree limbs, and floods, this quilt incorporated his favorite places and Ganesha, his remover of obstacles. It was made over a long period of auditioning fabric after fabric, using some and discarding others. It is pieced, appliquéd, fused, machine embellished, and machine quilted. I didn't paint any fabrics specifically for use in the quilt; instead, I chose each piece from the collection of my painted fabrics. The only exception is the Ganesha batik in the center of the quilt, which I purchased from Batik Tambal.

Point Bonita,
by Mickey Lawler,
28″ × 22″, 2008

■ I made *Point Bonita* to remember this bench where many good friends often sat to talk and watch the sun set on the Pacific. If you look closely, you can see the Farallon Islands in the distance—a sure sign of a clear night. This small quilt was hand and machine appliquéd, fused, and pieced. The slats on the bench were inked in last.

Dog Beach,
by Stevii Graves,
36″ × 21″, 2010

■ Stevii, an editor, author, and owner of My Needles & Notions (myneedlesandnotions.com), has been involved with quiltmaking since 1975. She has been a juror and judge for competitions throughout the United States and has been the judging coordinator for Road to California since 2002. She is owned by a very discriminating Papillon named Dani. Her quilt is hand and machine appliquéd and machine quilted.

African Reflections,
by Claire A. Wills,
34¼" × 24¼", 2010

■ A beautiful balance of sky, water, and land provides the background for Claire's interpretation of a photo taken on her latest trip to Africa. (See Designing from a Photograph or Illustration, page 72.)

Evening Sea, Morning Sky,
by Pamela T. Hardiman,
85″ × 85″, 2009

■ Some of Pam's hand-painted fabrics resulted in a beautifully straightforward abstract seascape. Pam paints on silks, cottons, and rayons for her business, Pamela T. Hardiman: Liturgical Fiber Art.

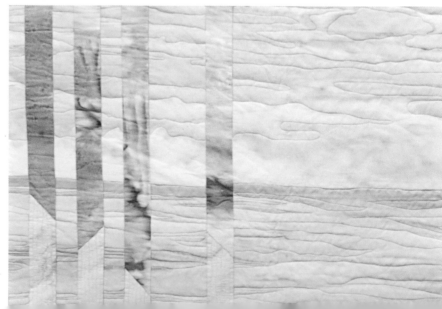

Agios Alexandros,
by Pamela T. Hardiman,
19″ × 36″, 2010

■ On a recent trip to Greece, Pam and friends visited a beautiful church near the Adriatic Sea. The church was privately built to honor a family's son, Alexander. Pam's quilt reflects the exquisite serene blue of both sky and water.

Meteora—Land of Mystery and Monks,
by MaryLyn Leander,
28″ × 40″, 2010

■ MaryLyn traveled to Greece with Pam
Hardiman and became enamored of the
brilliant red wild poppies that covered
the rugged hillsides of the Meteora
region. In the background, monasteries
perched on the tops of mountains in that
area seem to float in the sky. *Meteora* is
machine pieced and hand quilted.

A Quiet Walk, by Carole Carter,
33″ × 40″, 2010;
machine quilted by Elaine Gilbert

■ For her foreground, Carole chose a variety
of SKYDYES painted pieces that reflected
the colors in a sunset sky. She grounded the
design with a line of distant mountains. Carole
hand appliquéd all the sections and fused the
detailed trees and flowers.

Which One Is the Frog Prince?
by Jean Thibodeau,
34″ × 36″, 2002

■ Highlighting intriguing batik art from Batik Tambal, Jean surrounded the panel with hot and cool complements. A dark fabric with a moon (left center) is a piece by Terry Keenan that was painted on black pima cotton.

Shibam: Manhattan of the Desert,
by Trish Hodge,
35" × 34½", 2010

■ Trish used SKYDYES fabric for the clear blue sky and sandy-colored foreground. Then she collected a variety of other painted fabrics to give texture to her buildings. She designed this quilt using pictures. (See Designing from a Photograph or Illustration, page 72). The houses in the town of Shibam are all made out of mud brick. Incredibly, about 500 of them are tower houses that rise five to eleven stories high, with each floor having one or two apartments. These houses have been in existence for hundreds of years.

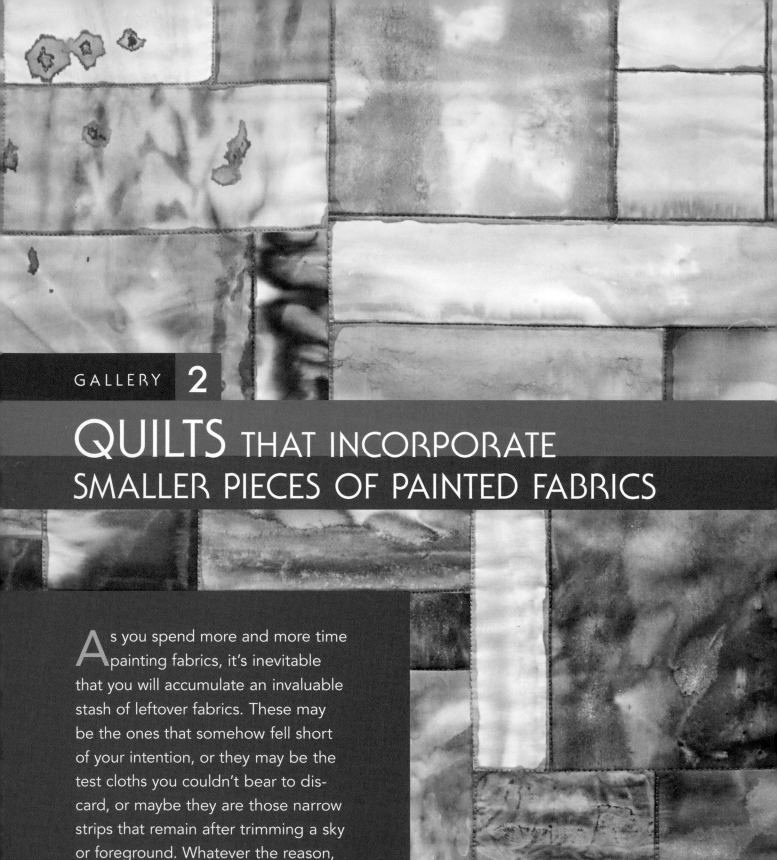

GALLERY 2

QUILTS THAT INCORPORATE SMALLER PIECES OF PAINTED FABRICS

As you spend more and more time painting fabrics, it's inevitable that you will accumulate an invaluable stash of leftover fabrics. These may be the ones that somehow fell short of your intention, or they may be the test cloths you couldn't bear to discard, or maybe they are those narrow strips that remain after trimming a sky or foreground. Whatever the reason, every inch of these orphan fabrics has potential to be the perfect piece in some quilt.

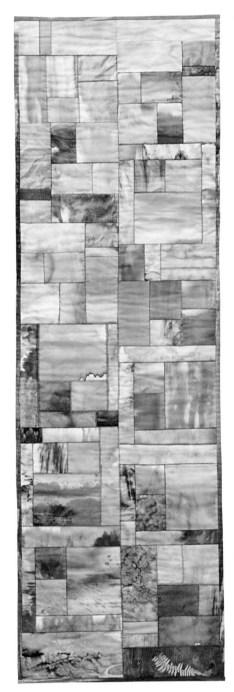
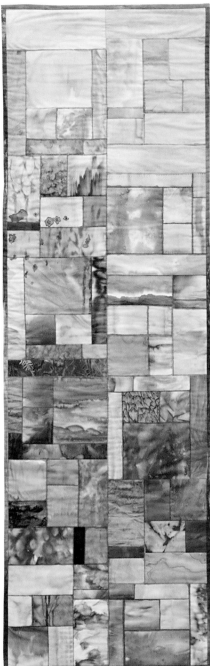

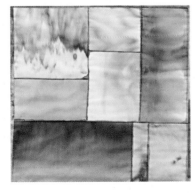

Tile Triptych,
by Mickey Lawler and friends,
each section 20″ × 64″, 2008

■ I designed two different square blocks for *Tile Triptych,* knowing
they could be rotated to offer a complex arrangement. I wanted
to use up many rather bland neutral-colored fabrics, interspersed
with tiny "keepers" here and there. I pressed my generous friends
into service to make as many blocks as they wished to add to the
piece. After the quilt tops were sewn, I emphasized the tile effect
by drawing grout lines with a gray paint marker.

Key West Sunset,
by Carole Carter,
89″ × 90″, 2008;
machine quilted by Elaine Gilbert

■ Carole Carter created *Key West Sunset* from pieces of SKYDYES fabric that she had collected. The quilt was inspired by a Kaffe Fassett design and the sunsets of Key West, Florida.

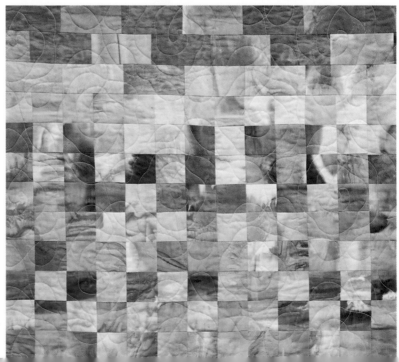

Color Squared,
by Carole Carter,
77″ × 83″, 2007;
machine quilted by Elaine Gilbert

■ Another of Carole Carter's beautiful quilts using leftover scraps of painted fabrics, *Color Squared* is a great example of juxtaposing bright colors with quiet colors for an energetic, dynamic design.

At a Crossroad,
by Claire A. Wills,
61¼″ × 60¾″, 2008;
machine quilted by Ann Marie Gontarz

■ In both *At a Crossroad* and *Let the Light Shine In,* Claire Wills created a sense of dimension through the placement of light and dark strips from her collection of SKYDYES fabric scraps.

Let the Light Shine In,
by Claire A. Wills,
53½″ × 54¼″, 2002;
machine quilted by Ann Marie Gontarz.

■ Claire's quilt is made entirely of painted scraps. A postcard of a quilt by Ursula Egger inspired this design.

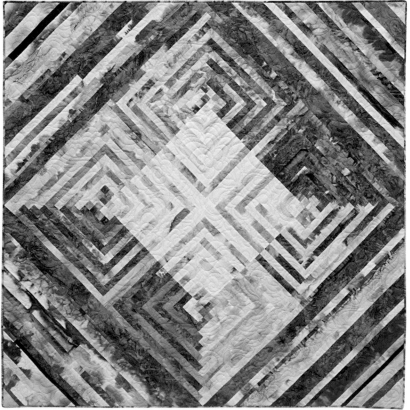

The Plaka,
by Jean Thibodeau,
105″ × 92″, 2007;
machine quilted by Tamni Tarr

■ *The Plaka,* constructed exclusively of painted pieces, reflects the mastery Jean possesses in creating beautiful art quilts from remnants. This quilt gives the impression of wet polished stone streets reflecting the night lights of a busy plaza. The design was inspired by the *Tile Triptych* (page 85) block patterns.

Grecian Waters,
by Jean Thibodeau,
16″ × 13″, 2010

Night Sky,
by Jean Thibodeau,
20″ × 20″, 2010

■ *Grecian Waters* and *Night Sky* are
small exercises highlighting painted
landscape fabrics that give the
viewer a sense of place.

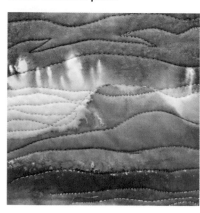

Beached,
by Jean Thibodeau,
24″ × 16″, 2007

■ Taking her lead from one piece of a SKYDYES seascape fabric, Jean embellished this small quilt with shells, threads, and beads to reinforce her theme.

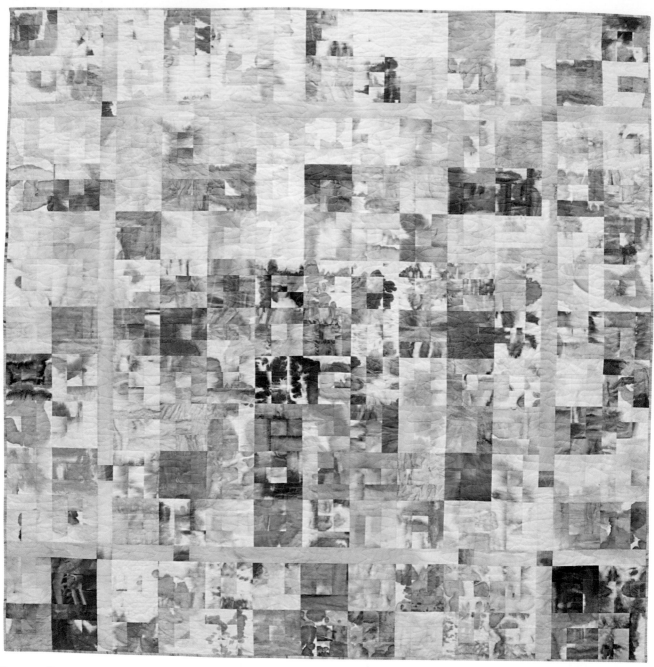

Summer II,
by Pamela T. Hardiman,
79″ × 79″, 2002;
machine quilted by Anne Marie Gontarz

■ Pam Hardiman's squares of painted
fabrics resulted in a joyous reflection
of the season.

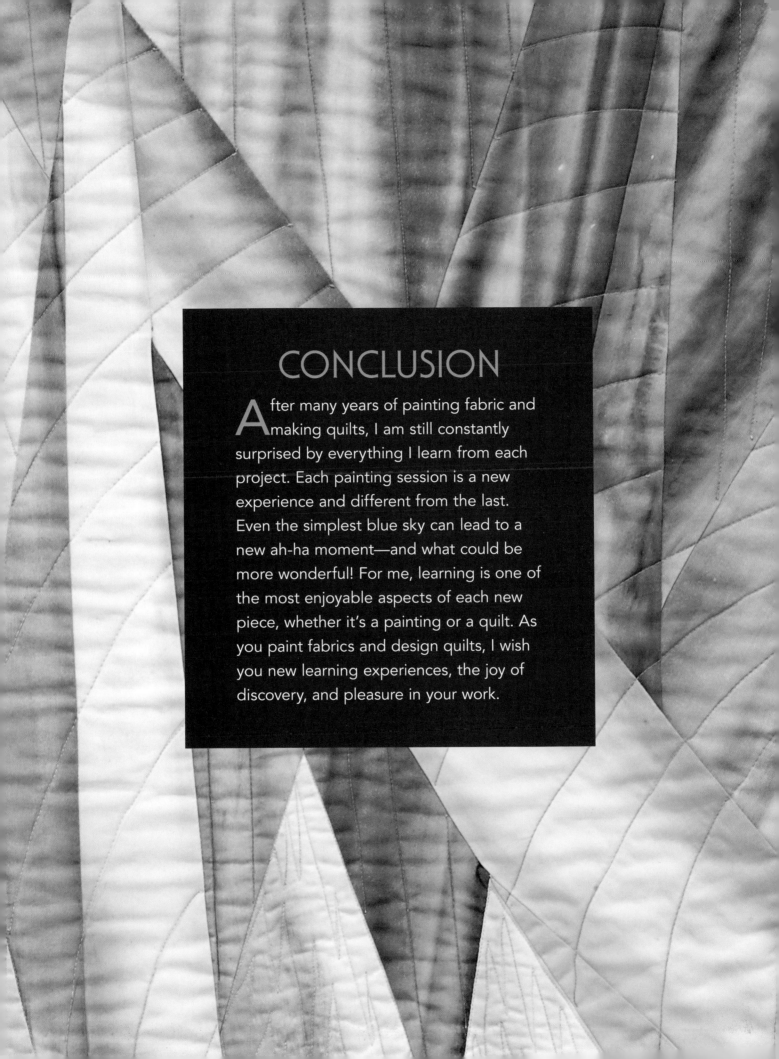

CONCLUSION

After many years of painting fabric and making quilts, I am still constantly surprised by everything I learn from each project. Each painting session is a new experience and different from the last. Even the simplest blue sky can lead to a new ah-ha moment—and what could be more wonderful! For me, learning is one of the most enjoyable aspects of each new piece, whether it's a painting or a quilt. As you paint fabrics and design quilts, I wish you new learning experiences, the joy of discovery, and pleasure in your work.

RESOURCES

PAINTS

Createx Airbrush Colors

www.dickblick.com

Liquitex Soft Body acrylic paint (opaque, transparent, and iridescent) and fabric medium

Find them at your local quilt or craft store or **www.ctpub.com**

Jacquard Transparent Textile Colors, Neopaque, and Lumiere (pearlescent)

Find them at your local quilt or craft store, at **www.dharmatrading.com**, or by calling 800-542-5227.

PROfab transparent paint, PRObrite pearlescent paint, and Pebeo Setacolor Transparent, Shimmers, and Opaque paints

www.prochemicalanddye.com or 800-2-BUY-DYE (800-228-9393)

100% COTTON FABRIC

Cotton Broadcloth Supreme #453

www.testfabrics.com or 570-603-0432

Patina PFD, Organic, Radiance cotton/silk blend (wholesale, or to find a retail store) **www.robertkaufman.com** or 800-877-2066

SEWING SUPPLIES

Thread, pins, needles, fusible web, rotary cutters, rulers, mats, scissors, and template plastic can be found at your local quilt shop. If one is not available in your area, check the following online businesses:

www.myneedlesandnotions.com

www.nancysnotions.com

ART SUPPLIES

Graph paper, X-Acto knife, stencil plastic or Mylar polyester film, natural sponges, Miracle Sponge, and stencil brushes can be found at your local art supply store. If you don't have an art supply store near you, there are several online:

www.cheapjoes.com

www.dickblick.com

www.jerrysartarama.com

www.pearlpaint.com

HANDPAINTED FABRICS BY SKYDYES

www.skydyes.com

QUILT DESIGN PROGRAMS

Electric Quilt Company

www.electricquilt.com

Mickey has been in demand by guilds and at conferences as an enthusiastic instructor of her serendipitous style of fabric painting for more than 20 years. Her workshop students work and play in a relaxed atmosphere that transcends simply learning technique. In her fabric paintings and her classes, Mickey emphasizes *collaboration with*, rather than *mastery over*, the medium. "The difference," Mickey says, "is that students create a personal fabric by learning to listen to the paints as they work and subsequently begin to welcome unexpected results not seen in the commercial fabric industry."

A lifelong resident of Connecticut, Mickey received her BA from the College of New Rochelle and her MEd from the University of Hartford. She has engaged in many independent art studies through universities and private courses. She lives in the town in which she grew up and continues to be inspired by the landscape of New England.

Visit Mickey's website at **www.skydyes.com**.

Mickey Lawler has been involved in quiltmaking since 1968 and is the creator of SKYDYES, a business specializing in her original hand-painted landscape fabrics. Her exhibits and awards for quilting and surface design have been numerous, including a recent retrospective of 23 of her quilts as a featured artist at the San Diego Quilt Show. Co-author of *Not Just Another Quilt* (Van Nostrand Reinhold, 1982) and author of *SKYDYES: A Visual Guide to Fabric Painting* (C&T Publishing, 1999), Mickey also has an instructional DVD (C&T Publishing, 2009), *Mickey Lawler Teaches You to Paint Landscape Fabrics*.

Also available by Mickey Lawler:

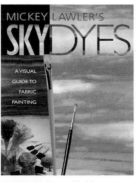

SKYDYES is available as an eBook and print on demand

Great Titles and Products

from C&T PUBLISHING and stashBOOKS.

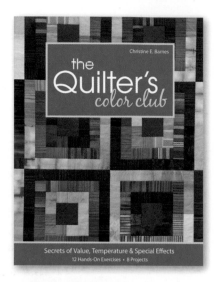

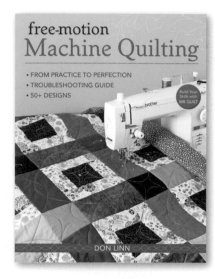

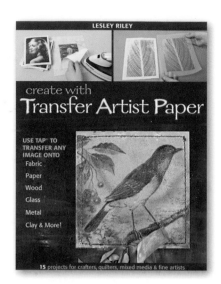

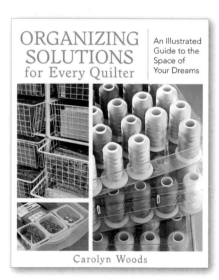

Available at your local retailer or **www.ctpub.com** *or* **800-284-1114**